KB079599

DUNAM CHOI ARCHITECT

DUNAM CHOI ARCHITECT

1987-2013

YOULHWADANG

DuNam Choi, Untitled. 2009. Oil on canvas. 60×60cm

To Kyungsun, for all her love and support

FOREWORD

Contemporary architecture on the Korean soil traces its genesis to the last decade of the 19th century, when the French catholic priest-architect Eugene Jean-Georges Coste and his fellow missionaries built a series of catholic churches including Myeong-dong Cathedral in Seoul. The collegiate Gothic buildings on the Yeonhee College and Ewha Women's College campuses designed by American and Canadian architects commissioned by the protestant missionaries soon followed, and so did several buildings for the Deoksugung Palace, and the Bank of Joseon building commissioned by Emperor Gojong. After the colonization of Korea by Japan in 1910, many public structures were built by the Japanese colonial government civil servant architects. Considering that when the first group of Korean architects educated at the Keijo (Seoul) Higher Technical School, predecessor of the Engineering College of Seoul National University, men such as Park Dong-Jin and Park Gil-Ryong, began their professional careers barely eight decades ago, what they built for the first private Korean clients, and what was happening in Europe and the United States were worlds apart, the trajectories of the architects practicing today in Korea may be characterized as having basically eliminated the perceived gap between the cutting edge and the acknowledged mainstream in architectural ideologies worldwide.

The architectural oeuvre of DuNam Choi may be characterized as being rooted in the mainstream Modernism of the 21st century. While some practitioners of his generation have veered off to formal experimentation of Post-modernism, Choi has firmly planted his formal reference in the international currents of architectural discourse. It may be said that his education in art at UC Berkeley of the late 1970's and in architecture at Harvard GSD of the early 1980's have molded the architect's unique sensibility toward the issues of the context, urban and natural, as well as his predilection for restrained yet elegant form-making.

DuNam Choi's own house in Buam-dong straddling the Joseon Dynasty fortification of Seoul, in spite of its relatively small size, amply demonstrates the architect's multi-faceted creative endeavor: a keen eye toward the topography and the natural vista; simple yet sculptural form; a limited palette of materials which, due to its earth-bound tessitura, imparts a certain sense of inevitability.

Among the architect's several mid-size output, the Gallery Samtuh in Cheongdam-dong may be considered to sum up DuNam Choi's architectural strategies well: in the urban setting where it is located, which is basically "anything goes" commercial landscape, the gallery has a strong presence; it has an adequate formal invention; the material for the building reads well, in spite of the fact that the Bace panel is reasonable in cost, due to its detailing, it comes across looking like limestone; the organization of interior spaces turn out adequately dynamic. Of his unrealized large-scale projects, a common thread may be found in DuNam Choi's sensitivity in analysis of the site, ingenuity of creating exterior space, use of pure geometrical surfaces in support of dynamic form. One would not hesitate to characterize DuNam Choi's architecture as very much being a part of the global discourse, while his sense of scale, proportion, and predilection for familiar textures, at the same time, make it a product of uniquely Korean sensitivity.

November, 2013
Seoul
Jong Soung Kimm

머리말

한국의 현대건축은 19세기 말엽 프랑스 가톨릭 사제이자 건축가인 외젠 장-조르주 코스트와 그의 동료 선교사들이 지은 명동언덕의 명동성당을 포함한 일련의 가톨릭 성당들에서 그 기원을 찾을 수 있다. 그 후 연희전문학교와 이화여자전문학교 캠퍼스 안에 개신교 선교사들의 의뢰로 미국과 캐나다 건축가들에 의해서 설계된 '대학 고딕 양식' 건물들과, 고종 황제의 의뢰로 설계된 덕수궁 안의 건축물 및 조선은행 건물이 뒤이어 지어졌다. 1910년 일제강점기가 시작된 이후 많은 공공건물들이 일본 식민정부의 공무원 건축가에 의하여 건설되었다. 한국 근대건축 역사에 있어 한국 초기 건축가 그룹의 일원으로 서울대학교 공과대학의 전신인 경성고등공업학교에서 수학한 박동진(朴東鎭)과 박길룡(朴吉龍) 같은 건축가들이 설계활동을 시작한 것이 불과 팔십 년 전이었고, 그들이 첫 세대 한국인 건축주들을 위해서 설계한 건물이 그 당시 유럽이나 미국에서 행해지던 건축과는 거리가 멀었던 것을 감안할 때, 오늘날 한국에서 활동하는 건축가들의 궤적은, 첨단과 세계 건축 이데올로기 주류 사이의 격차를 실제적으로 상쇄시키고 있음을 보여 주고 있다.

이런 관점에서 최두남(崔枓南)의 건축작품 세계는 21세기 모더니즘 원류에 근거하고 있다고 볼 수 있다. 그의 세대의 일부 건축가들이 포스트모더니즘의 형태적 실험으로 전향한 반면, 최두남은 자신의 지평을 국제적인 건축담론에 일치시키고 있다. 1970년대 후반 UC버클리대학교에서의 미술 수업과, 1980년대 초의 하버드대학교에서의 건축 수학은, 그로 하여금 컨텍스트, 그리고 도시나 자연에 연관된 의제들에 대하여 절제되고 우아한 형태를 지향하는 성향과 더불어, 그만의 독특한 감성을 형성하는 데 기여했다고 볼 수 있다.

그의 작업 중에서 조선시대에 구축된 서울 성곽을 면하고 있는 최두남의 부암동 자택은, 비교적 작은 규모임에도 불구하고 건축가의 다양하고 창의적인 노력을 충분히 보여 주고 있다. 지형과 자연풍광에 대한 예리한 안목, 단순하면서도 조각적인 형태의 사용 및 제한적인 재료의 취합 등은 땅을 지향하는 테시투라(tessitura)에 의해서 어떤 거부할 수 없는 필연성을 느끼게 한다.

그의 중규모 프로젝트들 중에서 청담동의 샘터갤러리는 최두남의 모든 건축적 전략들이 집약되어 있다고 할 수 있다. '모든 것이 난무할 수 있는' 상업화된 도심의 여건 속에 위치한 샘터갤러리는 강한 존재감을 표출하고 있다. 또한 그 건물에서 적절하게 표현된 역동적인 내부공간의 구성이라든지, 경제성을 고려한 외장 재료인 베이스패널의 사용이 섬세한 디테일을 통하여 석회암을 연상시키는 등, 각기 건물에 들어맞는 효과들을 연출하고 있다.

또 한편으로 최두남의 실현되지 않은 대규모 프로젝트에서는, 그의 대지에 대한 분석, 독창적 발상에 의한 외부 공간 창출, 역동적 형태를 추구하는 순수한 기하학적 면들의 사용 등을 통해, 그만의 감성적 연결고리를 발견할 수 있다. 이런 점에서 우리는 그의 건축이 세계적 담론의 일부로서 국제적인 흐름에 밀착되어 있음을 단언할 수 있는 동시에, 그 특유의 스케일 및 비례감과 친근함을 느낄 수 있는 재료의 구사를 통하여 독특하게 빚어진 한국적 감성의 산물이라고 규정지을 수 있을 것이다.

2013년 11월
서울에서
김종성

ARCHITECTURE

DUNAM CHOI'S HOUSES
YI EUISUNG

It has always been the aspirations of architects to envision and advocate for a total vision of their built environment. From the writings of Vitruvius to Palladio, from the works of Aalto to Wright, the comprehensive authorship of context, site, form, materials, furniture and details became an irrefutable responsibility of architecture. This creative and engineering ensemble provides the kinetic and narrative experience where art and design flourish within detail, surface, and space, to evoke a dialogue between patron, author and audience. Therefore, it is of no surprise that the spatial and theatrical nature of architecture was popularly termed the mother of all arts.

Unfortunately, this right of architecture to provide a total solution has rapidly eroded in recent years, especially in Asia and Korea. With the encroachment of separate disciplines (landscape architects, interior designers) and workscopes completed by different parties, the comprehensive vision gives way to a cluttered and compromised offering. This trend has been more acute in Korea where architects in big projects, executed by large faceless corporate offices, are losing ground. With an overwhelming dependency on financial returns and the rising power of the construction-development companies, architects have become mere illustrators and draftsmen. No longer are they tasked to envision a better environment that makes sense of the increasingly complex and layered modern existence. Rather, architects are tasked to the minimum denominator.

As the final line of defense against this catastrophic erosion of the architect's role in Korea, DuNam Choi anchors his practice by asking us all to remember what architects were called to do in the past. In a rigorous and defiant stance of the total vision, he advocates and insists in offering an updated Gesamtkunstwerk. The final stronghold is defined by single family private residences—a typology that historically has served the architect with the most intimate and immediate imprint of their design id.

In the mid 1800s the term Gesamtkunstwerk ("total work of art") was popularized by the composer Wagner to anchor his vision for unifying all the arts on the stage for his ambitious theatrical productions. The term began to evolve in parallel with the growth and transition of western cultural history from classicism to the modern era via the industrial revolution. As cities began to change radically with the intrusion of rural immigration, new mechanical transportation and factories, architecture underwent a radical transformation as well. With the waning of Neo-clas-sicism and the slow rise of industrial arts and abstract art, architecture began to be redefined by urban and socio-political forces. As architects searched for new modes of design and emboldened with the possibility of a new manifesto, the opportunity to redefine Gesamtkunstwerk became a very real proposition. One of the significant members of this movement is Henry van de Velde. Born in Bel-gium, Van de Velde would spend his formative years in Germany as the main figure of the Art Nouveau movement and later would recommend Walter Gropius to head the new institution that would become the Bauhaus.

The Art Nouveau movement, influenced by the Arts and Crafts Movement from the United States, defined a culture of design that aggressively extended the ar-chitecture into interior furnishings, details and finishes. Figures like C. R. Mack-intosh, and Greene and Greene designed everything from the structure to the door handles. Van de Velde's own house would mark one of the most significant project he would do and for the Gesamtkunstwerk movement. Not only was each room designed and crafted in the most intimate detail, he designed the dress that would be worn by his wife.

Gesamtkunstwerk continues with architects that define 20th century modernism: Alvar Aalto, Le Corbusier and Mies van der Rohe. These architects and countless others have pursued a holistic vision of their design, even designing fabric swatches and hardware details for their houses. Therefore, DuNam Choi is not defining a new paradigm but rather, is an heir to this important heritage in a mar-ket that has reduced the architect's role to a compositional draftsman. The Ko-rean architectural culture and market needs to be reminded of the architect's true and comprehensive role and DuNam Choi's advocacy for such workscope is exemplified by an examination of his residential projects.

This article will focus on three built residential projects of DuNam Choi that suc-cessfully showcase his "total design" and defiantly represent the call for com-prehensive design which are varied and testify to the architect's response to the client's desires and domestic culture, and the site. DuNam Choi's language is deeply rooted in very contemporary modernism where simple, strong and con-fident massing and organization becomes an appropriate system to address the issues of Korean residential urbanism.

I think the discussion of residential design should begin with the architect's own house, the Buam-dong House. The Buam-dong House encapsulates several key elements that structures Dunanm Choi's total design. There is no premeditated "style"; rather it's a careful examination of site opportunities, programmatic nar-ratives and understanding materiality and landscape that the house "emerges" from these conditions. The site is very unique. It is amazingly tight and difficult site, but is defined by a beautiful length of the city's ancient citadel wall. This triangular site borders on residual territory. The design overcomes the legal parameters, heightens the symbolic and historical relationship to the citadel wall that by virtue of the successful design, raises the awareness and significance of DuNam Choi's pursuit of his total design. The morphology of the house is site driven and context driven and is a deft choreography between the large site restrictions (and opportunities) with the internal domestic structure of the rooms and programs. The material choice is also well chosen as its monolithic and monochromatic characteristic of exposed concrete allows the richness of the citadel wall to express itself.

Additionally the relationship between family gatherings results in an intelligent organization that highlights the site. As one enters the gate, one is treated to a long linear exterior stairway that is the organizational spine of the house. It takes one past the second floor and all the way to the occupy-able roof that in essence absorbs and encapsulates the Buam-dong valley as a secondary living room. In this highly tense and dense matrix, the introduction of more materials on the exterior would have been excessive. Rather the intense passion and energy has been strategically been invested into the site plan and massing. Tactical energy is poured to clever details in hardware and interior design materiality, fixtures and furnitures. The house feels much larger than what the numbers and drawings suggest.

The relationship between inside and outside evolved further with the Pyeongchang-dong House. The Pyeongchang-dong House is three stories with a taut simple rectilinear massing. The parti is clear with three horizontal massing. The ground level is conceptually clear and transparent, rendering the second floor massing as an intentional solid where distinct window openings, either long horizontal bands or punched, are subtracted from this monolithic mass. The clear massing organization and exterior materials allow a cinematic relationship between building surface and exterior gardens, courtyards and other public spaces. But in reality, the rectilinear volume houses a three dimensional matrix of framing devices and moments. The assemblage of 3 dimensional gridding allows a dual reading of simple massing with complex relationships between interior spaces and their exterior views. The concept of blurring the inside and outside—which is one of the mainstay of modernism—is elevated to a necessity in the tight sites of urban Korea. This relationship between interior space and the exterior landscape mandates that the architect be the author of this dialogue and therefore the author of three scopes: the interior design, the filter (which is the house) and the landscape. Though this 3-layered design might be a given definition of an architect's role in the west, this level of design integration is difficult in Korea and accents DuNam Choi's adamant demand for total design. The framed views of the trees juxtaposed with the materiality of the exterior spaces act as a visual glue for the residents inside. The rich palette of finishing material resonates at an emotional level as framed compositions of landscape and hardscape are discovered.

The Hannam-dong House is the ultimate culmination of the issues explored in the Buam-dong House and an evolution and extension of the material and site relationships explored in the Pyeongchang-dong House. If the Pyeongchang-dong House is seen as a box on a flat site, the Hannam-dong house is a far more dynamic and ambitious work. The house offers rich site works that echoes the variety and textures of the much smaller Buam-dong House. The Hannam-dong House is a mature work that explores existing vernacular residential typology (the blank neutral walled and gated compound) that upon its entry, offers the visitor a different spatial and sensory experience through a narrative of circulation paths and landscape beauty for the eyes to feast on.

The oscillation between monolithic surfaces and its interruption with precise cuts and articulation provides this house with a multi-layered understanding of tectonics that are associated with issues of scale and connective details. Unlike the Pyeongchang-dong House where the relationship between interior and exterior can be appreciated by entering the house (even at the ground floor level), the Hannam-dong House begins this narrative the moment one enters the gate and before entering the house. In this regard, this shares the soul of the Buam-dong House where site strategies and landscape strategies blur and outline the total concept of the house before one enters the interior.

The materiality and the details are exemplary as DuNam Choi clarifies the role of the material (stone, metal and concrete) through precise intervening details. Concepts embedded in details and systems related to glazing elements and apertures are proportional to the larger gestures of the site plan and the relationship between the house and the site. The parti of the house plan not only express the internal organization of the family needs but is a deft collaborator with the landscape in creating a sequence of spatial courtyards. These spaces are not only symbolically relevant for the residents but they also act as avatar spaces of similar ritualistic spaces inside. To conjoin these two different sets of spaces, DuNam Choi relies on a careful rhythm of solid / void, hard massing / soft landscape and a selection of rich material palette (like the Pyeongchang-dong House) to anchor and lend identity to the spaces.

Looking at the series of unbuilt work reveals a more dynamic and bold interpretation of DuNam Choi's relationship to the site. In one example, the shardlike projects not only react to the density and randomness of the forest context but it was an emotional projection onto the site by DuNam Choi. In another, the long disciplined rectilinear bars and elements aim to frame larger portions of the site as if to enlarge the canvas the architect desired to conquer. Examining these projects clarifies the necessity of an integrated design especially between landscape and architecture. DuNam Choi's advocacy for total design is a matter of survival; a fight to save the creative and cultural aspirations of architecture in a market and society where those responsibilities are quickly eroding from the architects' hands.

Yi Euisung received his Bachelor of Architecture at Cornell University and his Master of Architecture at Harvard University. Yi has been involved with academia and scholarship for over fifteen years in Asia and the U.S. He is currently Principal of Morphosis Architects and director of the NOW Institute at UCLA., and an adjunct associate professor at USC School of Architecture.

최두남의 집
이의성

건축가들은 늘 자신의 총체적인 작업 환경을 열망하고 주장해 왔다. 비트루비우스와 팔라디오는 글을 통해, 알바 알토와 프랭크 로이드 라이트는 작품을 통해, 대지와 컨텍스트, 형태와 재료, 가구, 디테일을 아우른 총체적인 접근을 건축의 몫으로 포섭했다. 이런 창조적 공학적 총체성은 건축주와 건축가, 대중 간의 담론을 이끌어내고, 역동적이며 서술적인 경험을 제공한다. 그 경험 안에서 면과 공간, 디테일을 통해 예술과 디자인이 꽃피는 것이다. 이런 측면에서 건축의 공간적 연극적 특성이 예술의 원천으로 불리는 것은 당연하다.

그러나 안타깝게도, 건축의 총체적 권위는 최근 들어 급격히 쇠퇴했다. 특히 한국을 포함한 아시아 지역이 더욱 그렇다. 조경, 인테리어 등 건축 분야의 세분화가 발생하고 인접 분야의 작업 범위가 확장되면서 건축의 총체적인 시각이 크게 훼손되었다. 한국의 이런 현상은 대기업 주도의 대형 상업 프로젝트에서 더욱 심화되었다. 경제적 이윤을 좇는 건설회사와 개발사에 꼼짝없이 묶인 건축가는 삽화가나 제도가에 불과하다. 건축가는 더 이상 다양하고 복잡한 양상의 현대인 들에게 더 나은 환경을 제시하고자 일하지 않는다. 건축가에게는 최소 분모의 역할만 주어진다. 최두남의 건축은 건축가의 역할이 작아지는 한국 상황에 대한 마지막 변론이다. 그의 건축은 과거 건축가의 역할을 다시금 강조한다. 그는 엄격하고 저항적인 총체적 시각에서 새로운 '종합예술작품(Gesamtkunstwerk)'을 강하게 제안한다. 역사적으로 건축가의 디자인 정체성이 비교적 잘 반영돼 온 단독주택은 이를 위한 최후의 보루이기도 하다.

1800년대 중반 작곡가 바그너는 모든 무대예술을 통합하려는 그의 비전을 '종합예술작품'이라 명명했다. 이 명칭은 서구문명이 산업혁명을 거쳐 고전주의에서 근대로 전환되는 시기에 크게 진화했다. 농촌 인구가 도시로 유입되고 새로운 운송수단과 공장이 도시의 급진적인 변화를 야기하면서 건축도 크게 변하게 되었다. 신고전주의의 쇠퇴, 산업예술과 추상예술의 뒤늦은 발흥과 더불어 건축은 도시적 사회정치적 힘에 의해 재정의되었다. 새로운 디자인 방식과 선언의 가능성으로 건축가들이 대담해지면서 종합예술작품을 재정의할 기회를 갖게 됐다. 이런 움직임을 이끌던 사람 중 하나가 앙리 반 데 벨데이다. 벨기에 태생의 그는 독일 아르누보의 주요 인물로 떠올랐고, 후에 바우하우스가 될 학교의 교장으로 발터 그로피우스를 추천한다.

미국 미술공예운동의 영향을 받은 아르누보는 건축을 실내장식과 디테일, 마감의 영역까지 공격적으로 확장해 나갔다. 매킨토시나 그린 앤 그린 형제 같은 인물은 구조에서부터 문 손잡이까지 모든 것을 디자인했다. 반 데 벨데 주택은 가장 중요한 종합예술작품 중 하나다. 그는 각 공간을 정교하게 세부적으로 디자인했으며 심지어 아내의 드레스까지 디자인했다.

종합예술작품은 알바 알토, 르 코르뷔지에, 미스 반 데어 로에 등 20세기 모더니스트로 이어진다. 이들만 아니라 수없이 많은 건축가가 직물이나 철물 디테일 등을 포함해 토털 디자인을 지향했다. 그러니, 최두남이 새로운 패러다임을 정의하는 것은 아니다. 건축가의 역할을 구성적 제도공으로 축소시킨 현재의 시장에서 그는 중요한 과거의 유산을 계승하고자 하는 것이다. 한국의 건축문화와 시장은 진정한 건축가의 총체적인 역할을 다시 되새길 필요가 있다. 최두남의 일련의 주택 시리즈는 바로 그 역할과 작업을 옹호한다.

건축주의 다양한 요구와 주거문화, 대지에 반응하는 건축가 최두남. 이 글은 그의 토털 디자인을 실험적인 세 가지 주택 작업을 통해 들여다본다. 최두남의 언어는 수식 없이 강력하고 자신감있는 볼륨과 구조를 선보이는 현대적 모더니즘에 기원한다. 또한 한국 도시의 주거 문제를 고심하기에 적합한 소재이기도 하다.

그 논의는 건축가 자신의 부암동주택에서 시작된다. 부암동주택은 최두남식 토털 디자인의 주요 축약판이다. 의도적인 스타일 부재를 대신하는 대지에 대한 면밀한 관찰, 프로그램의 서술, 재료와 경관에 대한 이해로부터 집은 출발한다. 독특한 삼각형 대지는 매우 협소하고 어려운 조건이지만 한편으로는 아름다운 서울 성벽과 맞닿아 있다. 이 주택은 법적 변수를 극복하며 성벽과의 상징적 역사적 관계를 맺는 데 성공한다. 그러면서 토털 디자인의 중요성과 인식을 강화시킨다. 외부적으로 대지의 제약과 컨텍스트의 영향을 받으면서도 내부적으로 각 실(室)들과 프로그램 구조를 능숙하게 다루고 있다. 재료의 선택도 적절하다. 노출 콘크리트의 단색적 특징이 성벽을 더욱 풍부하게 만든다.

또한 가족이라는 관계를 통해 대지를 지능적으로 조직하고 있다. 대문을 들어서면 집의 중추 역할을 맡는 긴 외부 계단이 이층을 지나 옥상으로 이어진다. 옥상은 본질적으로 부암동 계곡을 또 다른 거실로 삼고 있다. 이처럼 긴장과 밀도가 엮인 상황에서 다양한 외부 재료는 과도한 선택이었을 것이다. 대신 그는 배치와 매스감을 깊게 고민하고 내부 철물 디테일과 재료의 물성, 가구

등의 디자인에 전략적으로 집중했다. 이 때문에 집은 도면이나 실제보다 더욱 크게 느껴진다.

평창동주택에서는 내부와 외부의 관계가 더욱 진화한다. 단순하지만 팽팽한 긴장 구조를 이루는 박스들로 구성된 이 삼층집은 세 개의 수평적 볼륨이 명확히 드러난다. 투명하고 깨끗한 일층에 비해 이층은 불투명한 매스에 수평으로 긴 창문을 냈다. 명확한 매스 구성과 마감 재료는 건물 표면과 외부 정원, 중정(中庭), 그리고 다른 공용 공간 사이에 드라마틱한 관계를 이뤄낸다.

그러나 현실에서 이 박스들은 삼차원적 틀과 틈새 속에 엮여 있다. 이 삼차원적 격자 집합으로 인해 이중적 해석이 가능하다. 매스는 단순 명료하지만 내부 공간과 외부 형태의 관계는 복합적이다. 모더니즘의 중심 테마이기도 했던 내외부 경계의 모호함은 한국 도시의 협소한 대지 상황에서 필요 불가결한 것이 되었다. 이를 구축하기 위해선 건축가가 실내, 주택, 조경 디자인의 주체가 되어야 한다. 서구에서는 이 세 분야를 모두 다루는 것이 건축가의 역할인 반면, 한국에서는 이런 통합적 접근이 어렵다. 이런 상황에서 우리는 역으로 토털 디자인에 대한 최두남의 단호함을 엿볼 수 있다. 외부 공간의 물성을 고스란히 보여 주는 이곳의 나무 프레임을 통해 거주자의 시야는 확장된다. 다양한 재료, 자연과 인조 경관의 구도가 인간의 정서를 자극한다.

한남동주택은 부암동주택을 통해 탐험한 문제들의 해답이다. 한편으로 평창동주택을 통해 모색한 재료와 대지 사이의 관계가 확장되고 진화한 것이다. 평창동주택이 평지에 상자를 배치한 것이었다면, 한남동주택은 그보다 훨씬 역동적이고 야심차다. 또한 부암동주택에서 보인 다양한 질감과 견줄 수 있는 풍부한 대지의 구축을 보여 준다. 한남동주택은 작가의 원숙한 작품으로, 막힌 담과 대문으로 이루어진 기존의 주거형태를 벗어나, 들어서는 순간부터 시선을 유혹하는 아름다운 풍광과 잔잔한 마당 길들을 통해, 다른 차원의 공간 및 감각적 경험을 맛보게 한다.

한남동주택은 규모와 연결의 문제를 단일한 면과 절개와 분절을 오가는 구성을 통해 다층적으로 풀어냈다. 내부와 외부의 관계를 경험할 수 있는 평창동주택과 달리 한남동주택에서는 대문을 들어서는 순간 집 안에서 이런 경험이 발생한다. 이는 부암동주택과도 상통한다. 대지와 주변 경관의 경계가 흐려지고 내부에 들어서기 전에 집의 총체적 개념을 이해하기 위한 서술이 시작되는 것이다.

최두남은 디테일 사이 각 재료들(돌, 금속, 콘크리트)의 역할을 정확히 이해하고 재료 간의 관계를 조직한다. 그렇기 때문에 그 질감이나 디테일은 본보기가 될 만하다. 창문이나 구멍 등은 배치 계획과 대지와의 관계성 같은 더 큰 형태에서 역으로 도출되어 세부적으로 디자인되었다. 평면은 가족들이 요구하는 내부 조직을 이루고 있을 뿐 아니라 주변 경관과 능숙하게 결합되어 중정의 시퀀스를 만들어낸다. 이 공간들은 거주자를 위한 상징적 공간이자 실내 공간의 분신이다. 이런 두 개의 다른 공간을 결합하기 위해 최두남은 세부 디자인과 다양한 재료의 사용에 주의를 기울여 공간에 정체성을 담는다.

완공되지 않은 최두남의 작업을 보면, 그가 대지와의 관계를 더욱 역동적으로 해석하고 있음을 알 수 있다. 예를 들면 양평주택에서는 문맥적으로 숲의 밀도와 임의성에 반응할 뿐만 아니라, 대지에 대한 최두남의 감정이 투사되고 있다. 또 다른 예로 조안리주택의 곧게 정렬된 가벽들과 요소들은 대지를 더욱 넓게 프레임하기 위한 것이다. 이는 더 넓은 캔버스와 대면하려는 건축가의 바람이다. 위와 같은 프로젝트를 살펴보면 지형과 건축 사이의 통합된 디자인이 필요함을 분

명히 알 수 있다. 최두남이 토털 디자인을 지지하는 것은 생존의 문제다. 건축가의 손에서 빠르게 떠나고 있는 창조적이고 문화적인 건축을 시장과 사회에서 잃지 않기 위한 노력이다.

이의성은 코넬대학교와 하버드대학교 건축대학원을 졸업했다. 십오 년간 미국과 아시아의 학문적 교류와 건축을 위해 광범위하게 활동했다. 현재 모포시스 아키텍츠의 총괄 책임자 및 UCLA의 NOW 인스티튜트의 디렉터, USC 건축대학교 겸임 부교수로 재직 중이다.

TOTAL DESIGN
PETER CHOI

A MODERN MOVEMENT

At another period in time, with the turn of the Industrial Age and under the guise of Art Nouveau, the arts freed themselves from the confines of Classical Symmetries. Forms were inspired by the curvaceous lines of nature and the organic form. Hector Guimard's Metro Stations for the Paris subways, Anton Gaudi's organic and mysterious apartments in Barcelona, and Charles Rennie Mackintosh's furniture and architecture for the Glasgow School of Art are all characteristic of the architecture and furniture design of the era. The innovative and daring jewellery and time pieces by Cartier, the colourful lamps and glass ware by Tiffany, and the iconic romance paintings of Gustav Klimt are all objects representative of the atmosphere of the time.

Designers and architects tried to harmonize their vision with nature. Design was no longer seen as split between the categories of textile design, industrial design, furniture design, graphic design and architecture. The different trades of design sought harmony with one another. Furniture was no longer seen as a later addition to architecture, but as a co-ordinated piece where one influenced the other. Curtains, drapes and wallpaper in living rooms were extensions of the architecture it occupied.

In Vienna at the turn of the nineteenth century, there was much discourse on and debate about architecture. Caught in the transition from Neo-Classicism and Modernism, the Viennese were deep in the so-called Secessionist Movement, their own version of the Art Nouveau school of thought.

However, in the architect Adolf Loos the design community had found an antagonist. Loos was busy decrying the florid excesses in embellishment of the Secessionist Movement. Loos was adamant that workers' time and energy should be spared of fiddling over decorative elements that would inevitably succumb to obsolescence and go out of fashion. And so, devoid of ornamentation and added decoration, Loos called for smooth surfaces that would be timeless and neutral. Minimalism was defined if not born.

Famously or infamously, architects know of the Austrian philosopher and thinker Ludwig Wittgenstein for his first adventure into architecture. In 1925, Wittgenstein's sister Margaret Storborough-Wittgenstein had hired architect Paul Engelmann to design a large townhouse in Vienna. Engelmann was designing a house composed of three white cubes after the modernist style of Adolf Loos.

Ludwig Wittgenstein who was working as a school teacher started to immerse himself in Engelmann's drawings. Slowly, Wittgenstein's considerable attention started to go into an excruciatingly lengthy period designing radiators, doors, door-knobs and windows. Wittgenstein effectively deconstructed the meaning of each and every part of and piece within the house. For example, for the windows he designed an iron-screen/curtain, weighing 150kg, that is lowered into the floor by steel chains and a counter-ballast. In the end, three years later, Wittgenstein's elder sister sold the house, before even living in it, as she felt the house was too austere.

Moving across the Atlantic Ocean, during the same period of Adolf Loos' eminence, one need only take a look at America's most famous architect Frank Lloyd Wright to understand the full impact of Art Nouveau. Wright was famous for the practice of "Full Design," developed in the spirit of Art Nouveau or Art Deco as it was also referred to with his projects, regardless of scale and programme.

He designed for a harmonization between humanity and nature. His most famous house, Falling Water, in Bear Run, Pennsylvania, epitomises an architecture and a nature that complements one another. While designing his houses, he would be sketching stained glass patterns for the windows, rugs, lamps, tables and even a dress for one of his clients. For the Johnson Wax Headquarters Building, he designed almost all of the office furniture and lighting elements within the cavernous headquarters building in Racine, Wisconsin. There was no doubt in Wright's world that all the disciplines of the arts would necessarily converge in his projects.

DOMESTICITY

DuNam's take on domestic architecture is to manifest the everyday rituals of living. Architecture is always subservient to the owner. The grandeur of the houses is thanks to the architect's consideration of the morning-to-night domestic pattern of the owners. Akin to Ludwig Wittgenstein's obsession with the meaning of the house and its constituent parts, the craftsmanship that DuNam Choi employs in his houses is born of the intensive thought and energy invested into the meaning of every element of the house: the front door, the fireplace, the kitchen, the dining area, etc. These are not rooms; they are places of daily ritual. Thankfully, one could argue that the devotion to such analysis of the elemental components of houses falls short of the excesses taken on by Wittgenstein.

A number of years ago, I had a conversation with DuNam about what defines "Korean-ness" in architecture. DuNam explained that even the most prosaic act, such as the dispensing of one's shoes from the parking garage into the split-level house at a lower level, and then having another shoe resource at the front door at an upper level, presents a unique dimension of "Korean-ness." As a new arrival to Seoul, I was hoping to gain an unusual insight into the culture of my new 600-year-old city. DuNam was speaking practically and, in fact, describing with utmost accuracy what it means to live in a Korean house.

VERTICAL LIGHT

One of the first challenges faced when designing a single-family home is usually the situating of the house on the land. Seoul being what it is, a hilly and mountainous terrain that runs into valleys and rivers, DuNam Choi tackled the positioning of the house in a very site-specific way; vertically. Given a virgin site in a densely built hilly area of Hannam-dong, DuNam Choi tackled, head on, the challenge of placing the house on this site, through a series of vertical interventions. Starting with the massive two-level podiums, defined by a handsome extruded cement panel wall lining the narrow street, two portals then mark the entrances at street level; one for a car and one for a formal entry. The formal entrance is defined by a grove of towering bamboo trees, stretching upward towards the sky. Like any proper gateway, the architect has marked the threshold by opening the view to the sky.

A graceful stairway, placed at right angle to the entry gate, takes the visitor to an a private garden courtyard at the upper level of the podium. With the informal functions of the house located at this level, for intimate family gatherings and outdoor entertainment. The formal part of the house takes the visitor one level above, to the top of the podium, where a graceful lawn dotted with red pine trees frames the view out to the city.

The spaces on this level are gathered in an "L" configuration around the garden. The grand and handsome white walls in the living and dining rooms are bathed in light due to the expansive windows that open to the south. Limestone floors flow out to the green lawn. If the sequence from the street to the garden, alongside the living level, was designed vertically, in order to follow the light, the character of these rooms has been designed horizontally, to breathe in the view and light from the garden and the surrounding city.

In continuing the theme of vertical light, a long two floor opening bordering the dining room brings in light from the linear skylight above. An industrial spiral staircase at the end of the linear space continues the family's circulation to the bedrooms at the upper level. The masterstroke of the Hannam-dong house is its singular use of light and space to thread the vertical circulation from the street below to the upper levels of the house.

A HOUSE TO CALL HIS OWN

For every architect, their day of reckoning arrives when they embark on designing their own house. Collapsing the roles of architect and owner into one body, the architect can only now wrestle with himself as to the aesthetic, programmatic, budget, scheduling, execution and delivery issues. And once built and occupied, the experience becomes arguably even more narcissistic, as he wakes up and confronts his own creation every day—be it good or bad. The most memorable and oft-cited case study is Frank Gehry's own San Diego house built 1977-78. Now legendary as the creative epiphany for a then corporate architect Frank Gehry, the role of architect-owner on his own personal project allowed him to follow through on his architectural curiosities, tendencies that were not permitted in his professional service role for his corporate clients.

TOUR DE FORCE

And so, based on that notion, a careful observation of Architect DuNam Choi's own 2000 designed residence in Buam-dong requires careful review, analysis and attention. One could argue that the basic tenets of DuNam Choi's domestic architecture and the architect's control of the process is evidenced in his house. It is in this house, that one may observe hints of the architect's future projects. Arguably, given the site's condition, programme and budget, it was the architect's most challenging project. It is only after having overcome the project's considerable challenges that he was able to go on to larger and more complex projects.

CONTEXT NEGOTIATION

Before all else, the design of any building must of course begin with its context. The Buam-dong site is blessed with three site characteristics: a hilly section, a medieval Seoul Fortress Wall and panoramic mountain views.

The windy, hilly drive up a narrow road between low houses seems to get narrower and steeper, verging on the claustrophobic, as one makes the approach to the house. Once in front of the house, the site becomes clearer. A man-made plinth or a platform, sitting on the foundation of a stone retaining wall, sets the stage for the house. A garden occupies the area behind the stone retaining wall at the lower end of the site. A gun-metal grey steel gate marks the entry at the top end of the street.

From the stone platform, the site ascends steeply to the old medieval fortress wall, defining the back edge of the site as running continuously past the mountain like a long train. The concrete house sits as a mediator between the street, the garden plinth and the hilly wall up to the back of the site.

DuNam Choi's first architectural move ostensibly separated and connected the house to the rear garden and to the medieval fortress Wall. By creating an exterior entry stairwell, between the newly designed sloped garden along the length of the Fortress Wall and the house, the staircase was able to negotiate both the house and the site, whilst creating a simple yet dramatic sequence within the house and garden.

By physically separating the volume of the house from the ground, condensation and water drainage issues were minimized and controlled. The Moabi wooden staircase brings the visitor from the sand-blasted steel gate at the stone platform to the concrete house entrance at midpoint, and then to the garden and the roof deck one floor beyond. Almost in mimicry of the arrival sequence to the house, one enters a modest exterior entrance at the gate. As one walks up the stairs, in line with a linear water pool marking the garden's edge, the sun and the view visually explode as one crests the stair at the roof deck. There, the sky becomes large and the surrounding mountains are thrown into sight.

SITE GEOMETRY

The medieval fortress wall sets the tone for the house and the site. With a garden, a linear water pool, and an entrance stairway running parallel to the wall, the street side of the property breaks from the rigidity and is made up of a sweeping, dynamic form. Sitting on a triangular plot of land, a split half circle was used to define the house's mass. The two sweeping arcs of the exposed architectural concrete street facade respond to the dramatic front-facing mountainscape of the valley below.

The sequence in and within the house is a procession that contrasts with the large sweeping mountain valley views to the front of the house, with the more intimate garden and medieval fortress views to the back. A vestibule made up of a wall with shoe storage greets the visitor to the house. A low slot opening tempers the view so as not to let the space seep beyond the entrance hall. Once inside the public areas of the house, floor to ceiling windows extend the space to the valley beyond. The back of the house below the exterior stair acts as the service zone with a linear kitchen. Punctuated views along the back wall frame the water feature, the garden and the medieval fortress wall outside. The unique qualities of the house were irrefutably inspired by the conditions of the site.

REPERTOIRE

DuNam Choi's architectural repertoire is varied. The act of procession into the house is a vital part of all his houses. The act of entering a space of a familiar domestic scale is pronounced within his sequences. Inevitably, most, if not all, of his houses are on hilly sites and necessitate a dramatic and clever vertical sequence. DuNam Choi's material palette is consistent throughout his work. From architecturally exposed concrete, to limestone, to slate and exotic wood, the natural make-up of the material is always assumed.

Walls become the animator of the architecture in this oeuvre. Walls are thin backgrounds for natural light or large art pieces. Walls become thick and compressed, to become service zones for storage and functional spaces. Walls become light and transparent, dematerializing man and nature.

DuNam Choi's houses are a composition of spaces. Perhaps, it is in this sense that DuNam Choi's work is about "Total Design." Much like Loos and his development of Raum Plan, walls signify the meaning of the programme it defines. These programmes are manifest in the dynamic spaces. The spaces interconnect and create a procession through the houses.

Peter Choi was educated at Cornell and Harvard Universities and trained at the offices of Skidmore, Owings and Merrill (SOM) and Richard Meier and Partners in New York. He is currently a Design Principal at Design Camp Moon Park (dmp) in Seoul.

토털 디자인
피터 최

모더니즘

산업혁명과 아르누보의 시대에 예술은 고전주의와 대칭의 속박에서 벗어났다. 자연과 유기적 곡선의 영향이 강했는데, 엑토르 기마르의 파리 지하철역, 안토니오 가우디의 바르셀로나 아파트, 찰스 레니 매킨토시의 글래스고 예술학교 건물과 가구 등이 대표적이다. 또한 카르티에의 보석과 시계, 티파니의 조명과 유리제품, 구스타프 클림트의 로맨틱한 그림도 잘 알려진 예다.

디자이너와 건축가는 자연과 조화를 이루고자 했다. 디자인은 더 이상 직물, 산업, 가구, 그래픽, 건축 등으로 분류되지 않고 하나의 조화를 추구했다. 가구는 나중에 첨가되는 것이 아니라 건축과 서로 영향을 주고받으며 조화를 이루는 요소가 되었다. 거실의 커튼, 휘장, 벽지는 건축의 연장이었다.

19세기 빈은 건축에 대한 담론과 논의로 가득했다. 신고전주의와 모더니즘의 전환기 사이에서 아르누보와 비슷한 성격의 분리주의가 진행되고 있었다. 하지만 아돌프 로스는 이같은 디자이너들에 대적하며 분리주의의 화려하고도 과도한 장식을 비판했다. 장식을 위해 시간과 에너지를 소모하는 것을 단호하게 비판했다. 그는 장식 없는, 영원하고 중립적인 매끈한 표면을 추구했다. 미니멀리즘의 기원이라 할 수 있다.

오스트리아 철학자 루트비히 비트겐슈타인의 건축 작업은 건축가들에게 잘 알려져 있다. 1925년 그의 누이 마가렛 비트겐슈타인은 건축가 파울 엥겔만에게 별장 설계를 의뢰했고, 엥겔만은 아돌프 로스의 모더니즘에 입각해 흰 입방체로 집을 구성하고 있었다.

당시 선생이었던 루트비히 비트겐슈타인은 엥겔만의 드로잉에 몰두하기 시작했다. 이어서 그는 난방기, 문, 문고리, 창문 등을 디자인하는 고통스럽고 긴 과정에 몰두했다. 그는 효과적으로 집 내부에 있는 각 개체의 의미를 해체했다. 창문의 경우 백오십 킬로그램의 철제 커튼이 강철 체인과 무게추로 바닥에 내려져 있다. 삼 년 후 루트비히 비트겐슈타인의 누이는 지나치게 간결하다는 이유로 살기도 전에 이 집을 팔아 버렸다.

아돌프 로스와 같은 시기 대서양 건너에서는 미국의 프랭크 로이드 라이트가 아르누보의 영향력을 과시했다. 라이트는 규모와 프로그램에 무관하게 아르누보의 정신을 이어받아 총체적 디자인(또는 아르데코)을 실천했다.

그의 디자인은 인간과 자연의 조화를 추구한다. 낙수장(落水莊)은 건축과 자연의 조화를 보여 주는 전형이다. 그는 주택을 설계하면서 창문 스테인드글라스의 패턴, 깔개, 조명, 테이블, 심지어 드레스까지 디자인했다. 존슨 왁스 본사의 경우에는 사무가구와 조명 모두를 디자인했다. 즉 라이트의 프로젝트에서는 모든 예술 분야가 융합되어야 했다.

가정생활

최두남에게 주거건축은 삶의 일상적 의식(儀式)을 명시하는 것이다. 건축은 주인을 위한 것이다. 위대한 집은 건축가가 건축주의 일상을 고려함으로써 성취된다. 루트비히 비트겐슈타인이 집착했던 개체의 의미에 영향을 받은 최두남은 정문, 벽난로, 부엌, 식당 등 집의 각 요소에 생각과 에너지를 불어넣는다. 이들은 방이 아니라 일상적 의식의 장소들이다. 개체에 대한 그의 분석은 다행히도 루트비히 비트겐슈타인의 과도함보다는 덜하다.

일전에 최두남과 건축의 한국성에 대해 대화를 나눈 적이 있다. 그는 집으로 들어오면서 신발을 갈아 신는 지극히 평범한 행위마저도 한국성으로 설명했다. 서울에 처음 온 나는 육백 년 역사의 도시문화에 대한 특이한 통찰력을 기대했었다. 최두남은 실질적이고 사실적으로 한국적 집에 사는 것이 어떤 것인지에 대해 말하고 있었다.

수직적 빛

단독주택 디자인에서 첫번째 과제는 주택이 지어질 대지를 구획하는 일이다. 이곳은 언덕이 강과 만나는 곳이다. 최두남은 그것을 고려하기보다는 주어진 대지의 특성을 수직적으로 해석했다. 주어진 대지는 언덕에 건물이 밀도 있게 들어선 한남동이다. 그는 수직적 중재를 통해 대지에 건물을 올려놓았다. 레벨 차를 갖는 거대한 볼륨의 두 단은 좁은 거리와 경계를 짓는 압축 시멘트 패널에 의해 윤곽이 드러난다. 두 입구는 거리 레벨에서 출입이 가능하다. 하나는 자동차를 위한 것이고 나머지는 주출입구다. 주출입구에는 우뚝 솟은 대나무 숲이 있다. 다른 곳과 마찬가지로 하늘이 보이게 천장을 뚫어 출입구임을 표시했다.

입구 오른쪽으로 우아한 계단이 있다. 계단을 오르면 단 위의 정원으로 갈 수 있고, 이층에 있는 정원은 가족 모임이나 외부 활동을 위해 사용된다. 다시 한 층 위로 올라가면 가장 위의 단으로 갈 수 있는데, 그곳은 잔디와 붉은 소나무가 있고, 도시를 내다볼 수 있다.

이 레벨의 실내 공간은 정원 둘레에 L자 모양으로 배치돼 있다. 거실과 식당의 웅장하고 멋진 흰색 벽은 남쪽 창을 통해 들어오는 빛에 휩싸여 있다. 석회석 바닥은 초록색 잔디로 흘러나온다. 거리부터 정원, 거실 레벨의 정경이 빛을 따라서 수직적으로 디자인되어 있다면, 이 방의 성격은 정원과 도시의 시각과 빛 안에서 호흡하기 위해 수평적으로 디자인되었다.

수직적 빛의 테마는 식당을 따라 난 보이드(void)와 채광창으로 쏟아지는 빛으로 계속 이어진다. 그 공간 끝에 위치한 산업적인 나선형 계단은 위층에 있는 침실로 동선을 이어 준다. 한남동주택의 주요한 성과는 거리에서부터 주택의 상부까지 수직적 이동을 연결하기 위해 빛과 공간을 독자적으로 사용한 것이다.

자기 자신의 집

건축가가 자신의 집을 설계한다는 건 바로 심판의 날을 의미한다. 건축가이자 의뢰인으로서 건축가는 미학, 프로그램, 예산, 일정, 실행 등 모든 방면에서 자신과 씨름해야 한다. 완공 후 거주하면서 매일같이 자신의 창조물을 보는 것은 (그것이 잘 됐건 잘 안 됐건) 자기애적인 경험이다. 가장 잘 알려진 경우는 프랭크 게리가 1977−1978년에 샌디에이고에 지은 자신의 주택이다. 당시 상업 건축가였던 게리는 다른 의뢰인을 대할 때 시도할 수 없었던 건축적 호기심을 자기 자신의 프로젝트를 통해 구현했다.

역작

이런 측면에서 2000년에 지은 최두남의 부암동주택을 주목할 필요가 있다. 주거건축에 관한 그의 기본 신조나 과정에 대한 통제뿐 아니라 건축가의 미래 프로젝트에 대한 암시를 발견할 수 있다. 대지, 프로그램, 예산을 고려했을 때, 이는 건축가에게 가장 어려운 프로젝트였을 것이다. 이런 어려움을 겪은 후에 그는 더 크고 복잡한 프로젝트를 수행할 수 있게 됐다.

맥락의 절충

건축은 지역의 맥락에서 시작된다. 부암동 부지에는 세 개의 장점이 있다. 언덕 지형, 서울 성벽, 파노라마 같은 산의 경치가 그것이다. 낮은 집들 사이로 난 좁은 길은 부암동주택에 가까워질수록 점점 더 좁아지고 가팔라져서 밀실공포증마저 느끼게 한다. 집 앞에 다다르면 대지는 뚜렷해진다. 석조 옹벽 기초에 기단은 집의 무대다. 옹벽 뒤 부지의 낮은 쪽에는 정원이 있다. 짙은 회색빛의 철제 대문은 길의 끝 꼭대기에 입구를 표시한다. 부지는 석조 기단에서 부지 뒤쪽 경계를 이루며 산 너머로 이어지는 서울 성벽까지 가파르게 오른다. 노출 콘크리트 주택은 길, 기단 정원,

대지 뒤쪽까지 닿는 험한 벽을 중재한다.

최두남은 우선 뒷마당과 성벽을 집에 연결하기도, 분리하기도 한다. 성벽을 따라 새로 만들어진 경사진 정원과 집 사이에 놓인 외부 출입 계단은 집과 정원에 간결하지만 극적인 시퀀스를 만들면서 집과 대지를 절충한다. 집을 땅에서 물리적으로 분리함으로써 결로와 배수 문제를 최소화하고 통제할 수 있다. 모아비나무 계단은 모래분사 가공 처리된 석재 기단 위의 철제 대문과 집의 현관, 나아가 정원과 위층의 지붕까지 연결한다. 집에 도착하는 시퀀스와 마찬가지로, 대문은 절제되어 있다. 정원 경계의 선형(線形) 못과 나란히 놓인 계단을 따라 지붕까지 오르면 태양과 주변 광경이 시각적으로 폭발한다. 꼭대기에 서면 커진 하늘과 주변을 둘러싼 산을 마주할 수 있다.

부지의 기하학

성벽은 집과 대지의 분위기를 고조시킨다. 정원, 선형 못, 벽과 나란히 놓인 출입 계단, 길 쪽으로는 역동적으로 휘도는 형태가 드러난다. 삼각형 대지에 놓인 반원이 집의 볼륨을 정하고 파사드의 두 반원이 전면에 펼쳐진 산의 경관에 대응한다. 내부로 들어가는 시퀀스는 전면의 확 트인 경관과 후면의 아늑한 정원, 성벽과 대조를 이루는 모양이다. 현관의 벽은 신발장이다. 낮고 좁은 창문은 공간이 입구 밖으로 새어나가지 않도록 시야를 제한한다. 집 내부의 공동공간으로 들어가면 전면 창 너머로 시야가 계곡까지 확장된다. 집 뒤쪽 외부 계단 아래는 선형 부엌을 포함한 식당이 있다. 뒷벽을 따라 멈춰진 시선은 야외의 수공간(水空間), 정원, 성벽으로 이어진다. 이 집의 독특함이 부지의 조건에서 비롯되었음을 명확히 알 수 있다.

레퍼토리

최두남은 다양한 건축적 레퍼토리를 사용한다. 집으로의 접근은 그의 주거건축에서 중요한 부분이다. 그가 만드는 일련의 장면은 주거공간의 규모로 들어가는 행위를 명시한다. 그가 설계한 집들은 언덕진 지형에 놓여 극적인 수직적 시퀀스를 갖는다. 또한 그는 여러 작업에서 일관성있게 재료를 사용한다. 노출 콘크리트와 석회석, 슬레이트, 이국적 목재 등을 아우르는 재료의 구성은 항상 등장한다. 이 작업에서 벽은 건축에 생동감을 부여한다. 벽은 자연광이나 예술작품의 얇은 바탕이 되며, 기능적 프로그램으로 두껍게 꽉 차기도 하고, 인간과 자연을 비물질화하며 가볍고 투명하게 되기도 한다. 최두남의 집은 공간들의 구성이다. 그의 작업이 토털 디자인인 것은 이런 면에 기인한다. 로스의 '라움 플랜(Raum Plan)'처럼 벽은 프로그램의 의미를 표명하고 프로그램은 역동적 공간에서 뚜렷해진다. 공간들은 서로 연계되고 집을 통해 행렬을 만들어 간다.

피터 최는 코넬대학교와 하버드대학교를 졸업한 후, 뉴욕 SOM과 리처드 마이어 사무실에서 건축실무를 익혔다. 현재 디자인캠프 문박 디엠피의 디자인 총괄을 맡고 있다.

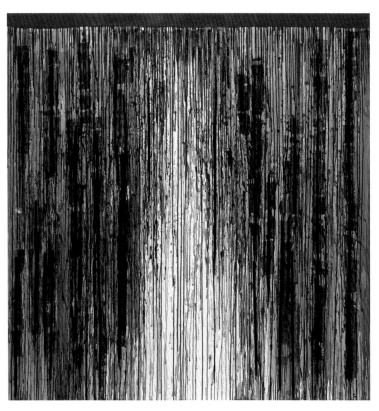

Untitled. 2012. Oil on canvas. 164×168cm

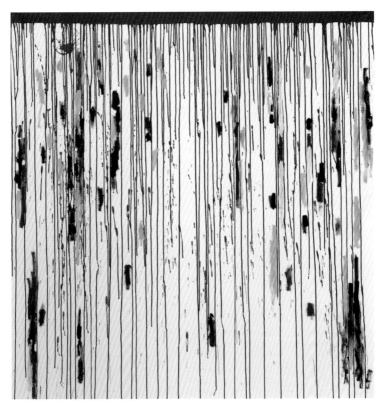

Untitled. 2012. Oil on canvas. 164×168cm

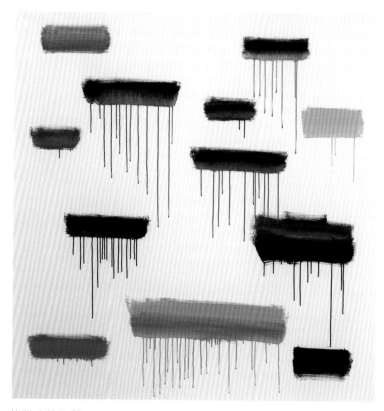

Untitled. 2012. Oil on canvas. 164×168cm

Sweet Encounter I. 2012. Oil on canvas. 164×168cm

Sweet Encounter II. 2012. Oil on canvas. 164×168cm

Untitled. 2012. Oil on canvas. 164×168cm

TOWARD AN ARCHITECTURE OF
SUBSTANCE AND GRAVITY

Eye of the storm—It is a spirit, alive amidst a purifying silence and accompanying bursts of energy and heat. But violent waves and isolated silence by themselves do not signify much. Unless that show of force stems from an intrinsic order from within, that expression of brute force is nothing but chaos.

I am soaked to the core in the process of searching for the eye of the storm. For the harvest of a few prized kernels of truths, countless seeds are cast and in tenacious pursuit of a concept, distracting confusions and temptations give away and float up, leaving only the crystalline silence as sediment. At last, I could forget the depth of this clear water.

Architecture is a task that seeks to provide the ripe conditions for experiences of lives to freely unfold; Space is architecture's medium and these conditions are both physical and metaphysical. The process of architecture projects the dynamics between the physical manifestations and the invisible forces behind onto the coordinates of time and space.

These interplays are further developed with sensibilities and realized with intellects. Without this entire progress, the tension one feels from an architectural model lacks the crucial depth. Moreover, space presented in simplistic order becomes predictable and in losing the potential for tension, becomes static. It's as if a masterful mystery novel lures the reader into the wee hours of the night. Elaborate composition and plot compensate for the limited number of suspects and make guessing the outcome anything but an impossible a task. Lucid space manifested within restraints stimulate the senses and incites the intellect to lead us into the world of experiences, Richness of this kind of experience is directly proportional to the depth of thinking and sensibility went into making of that space. Consider a wooden board lying on the ground. When that same board is hung high up in the air to become a diving board, it is no longer the same object. The diving board afloat in space transcends the two dimensional dynamics of a flat board in ground.

Beauty that is peculiarly Korean is called "meot," roughly meaning, grace, zest, gusto, kick. This beauty cannot be achieved without knowing the whole. Because without knowing the whole, the part cannot be deciphered. To decipher the part, one has to be enlightened. To be enlightened, one has to be filled with the possibility of the whole. Ultimately, truly meaningful beauty emanates from the confidence of knowing the totality and the exercise of deliberate restraint. In this process, one needs the keen insight to see the tree and the forest at the same time.

Modern time is the locomotive that is speeding along a tract with a desire to be free, discontinuity and severance, explosion and rupture. I lift up the board from the ground and start the climb towards the diving board. The urge to be soaked thoroughly again cannot be measured just as the height of the diving tower cannot be. I could only hope that the determination and the stamina of a marathoner will eventually lead me into the eye of the storm.

DuNam Choi

파장이 이루어낸 투명한 침묵

태풍의 눈—엄청난 에너지와 열기를 동반한 채 정제된 침묵 속에 깨어 있는 혼이라 할 수 있다. 그러나 격렬한 파장과 단절된 정적 그 자체는 별 의미가 없으며, 내재한 질서로 가늠되지 않는 힘만의 돌출은 혼돈일 뿐이다.

나는 태풍의 눈을 찾아 들어가는 과정에서 흠뻑 적셔진다. 몇몇 들어찬 알맹이를 찾기 위하여 수많은 씨를 띄우며, 개념을 향한 집념 속에 쇠약해진 많은 혼란과 유혹은 수면으로 떠오르고 소금기에 절여진 투명한 침묵이 남게 된다. 그제서야 나는 이미 해맑게 투명해진 물의 깊이를 잊을 수 있게 된다.

건축은 공간이라는 매개체를 통하여 경험을 유발시킬 수 있는 여건을 마련하는 작업이다. 이 여건은 물리적인 것과 형이상학적인 것을 포함할 수 있어야 하며, 이 과정은 외형상으로 나타나 있는 물리적인 현상과 표피 속에 내재한 보이지 않는 힘들의 역학을 시간과 공간이라는 좌표에 투영시켜 감성으로 현상하고 지성으로 인화해내는 작업을 거치게 된다.

따라서 이러한 과정이 결여된 상태로 조형에서 느껴지는 긴장(tension), 그 자체가 건축적 표현의 전부가 되어서는 깊이를 잃는다. 또한, 공간 전개에 있어 단조로운 질서로 다져진 연출은 추리가 가능하며 긴장의 잠재성을 잃고 만다. 그러나 등장인물은 한정되어 있으면서 치밀한 구성을 통하여 예상을 불허하는 추리소설 읽는 이로 하여금 밤을 밝히게 하듯이, 전체 속에 나타나 있는 공간의 명료성과 생동감 넘치는 풍부한 서정성은 감각을 자극하고 지각을 충동하여 우리를 경험의 세계로 인도하게 된다. 이 경험의 풍부함은 공간 뒤에 숨어 있는 사고의 깊이에 비례하여 사물에 대한 다원적 시각을 필요로 한다. 땅에 놓인 널빤지가 허공에 매달린 다이빙 보드(diving board)가 되었을 때 그것은 이미 같은 물건이 아니다. 공간 속에 띄워진 다이빙 보드는 이미 이차

원의 다이내믹을 넘어서 있기 때문이다.

한국의 독특한 미(美)를 '멋'이라고 표현한다. 이는 실제로 파격의 미일진대, 전체를 알고 있지 않으면 부분을 깰 수가 없으며, 깨기 위해서는 깨어 있어야 하며, 깨어 있기 위해서는 차 있어야 한다. 결국 진정한 의미에서의 멋은 전체를 알고 있는 여유와 절제 안에서 나올 수 있는 것이며, 이 과정에서 나무와 숲을 동시에 볼 수 있는 혜안이 필요하게 된다.

자유로워지고 싶은 욕망, 분절과 단절, 파열과 균열, 현대는 이 모든 것을 싣고 달리는 기관차. 나는 다시 땅에 놓인 널빤지를 집어 들고 다이빙대를 오르고 있다. 다시금 흠뻑 적셔지고 싶은 욕망은 얼마를 올라야 할지 탑의 높이를 알지 못한다. 다만 마라토너의 집념과 스태미너가 나를 마침내 태풍의 눈 속으로 인도하기를 바랄 뿐이다.

최두남

Untitled. 2013. Oil on canvas. 120×152cm

Untitled. 2013. Oil on canvas. 97×130cm

Untitled. 2013. Oil on canvas. 120×152cm

Untitled. 2013. Oil on canvas. 120×152cm

ARCHITECTURE

BUAM-DONG HOUSE

BUAM-DONG HOUSE

Buam-dong, Seoul, 2000

The Buam-dong House is situated on a unique triangular lot with a historical citadel wall in the back of the site. While designing a family house adapting to the complicated site conditions, a primary design concern was to remain sensitive to the historic citadel wall. The design process manifested as a series of trials and errors, hampered by site-related constraints through each iteration. In order to overcome these obstacles, it was necessary to use design as tour de force rather than yield to site related constraints.

After numerous trials, final design decisions resulted in a simple yet dynamic volume that conformed to the constraints of the site. The volume which is on a piloti floats as a horizontal layer that follows the contour of the site boundary, with a sense of liveliness.

In this project, priority was given to the establishment of spatial order based on flexibility and diversity in the interior space, which was treated as a single entity with sliding and folding doors which allow an uninterrupted spatial flow within the house.

The main entrance to the house can be accessed via a stairway anchored between the citadel wall and the house. Once inside the house, the circulation flows north to south, capitalizing on the same directional axis of the site.
All in all, the Buam-dong House is not only a result of a rigorous design efforts, but also a testament of a successful compromise between the site constraints and the architectural explorations.

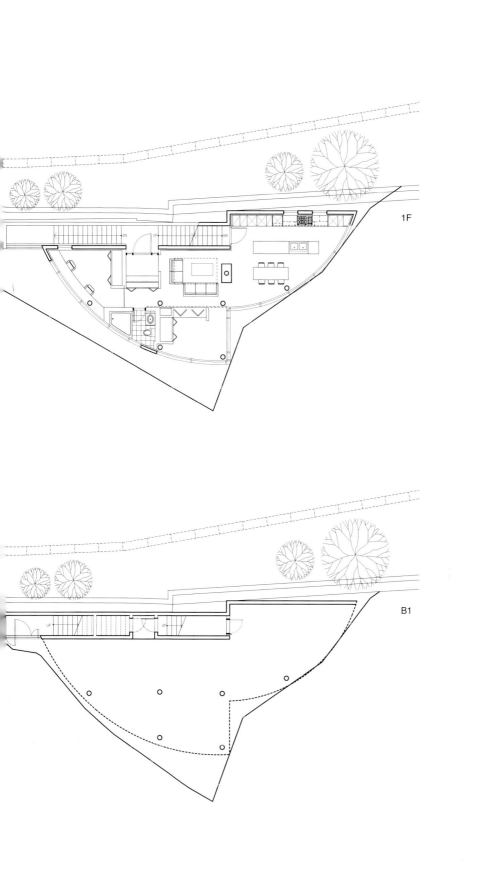

1F

B1

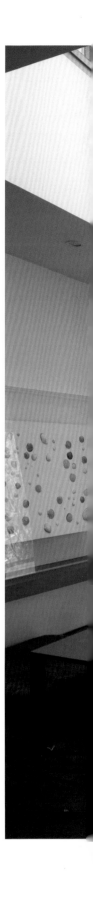

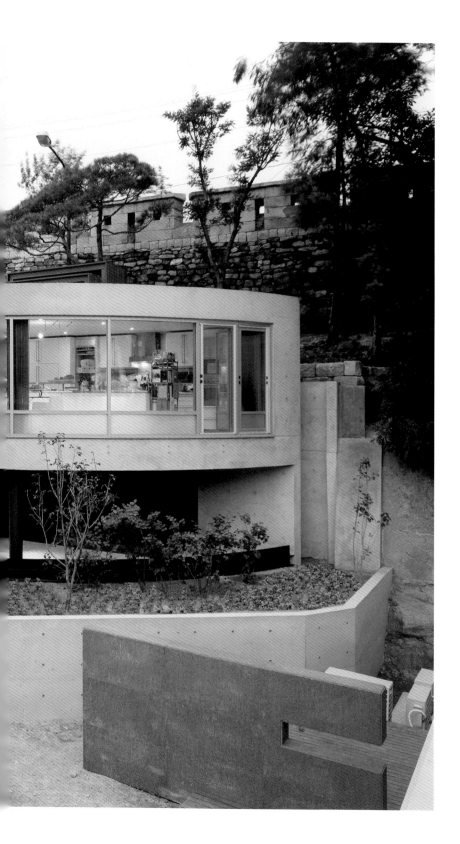

HANNAM-DONG HOUSE

HANNAM-DONG HOUSE

Hannam-dong, Seoul, 1997

Located on a residential street that looks onto charming sceneries, the site was located on a vacant lot, an exclusivity for the neighborhood. Due to the substantial height differences, there was a need for two accesses from the upper and lower part of the site. Designing this house was a challenge on two levels. One of the challenges was addressing the special relation and harmony between the building and the site as to secure an inviting interior and exterior space. The second issue concerned with the client's request to create a comfortable home for the family and not for public display. One strategy was to create two entrances on the upper and lower part of the site and to divide the site vertically, where the supporting programs including the garage are in the basement levels 1 and 2 while the living room, dining room, kitchen, and the guestroom are on the main level with the private spaces like the bedrooms, study, and the family room on the second floor. The design intent was to create a smooth and continuous spatial transition through natural light and varied scenic views from each room while offering comfort through timeless elegance.

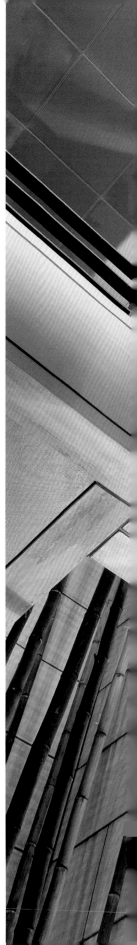

PYEONGCHANG-DONG HOUSE

PYEONGCHANG-DONG HOUSE

Pyeongchang-dong, Seoul, 2009

Due to the site condition where three sides of the lot were surrounded by neighboring houses, it was necessary to come up with a design where it was permeable enough for viewing opportunities and at the same time enclosed for privacy. One enters the house through an entry courtyard, which acts as a reference point where one can experience the unfolding of the spaces. Horizontal bands of wood siding over the stone façade unite the massing and modulate the scale of the house.

P-PROJECT

P-PROJECT

Pyeongchang-gun, Gangwon-do, 2006
Associated Architect: Samoo Architects

The first significant factor to consider when designing a building set in nature is its siting, like in the case of Pyeongchang Condominiums. The design challenge was trying to create a harmonious balance between an ambitious-scale building with the graceful profile of the mountains, animated by steep hillsides and flowing valleys. In its form, the horizontal building mass, gracefully positioned in front of the valley, is elevated by a row of pilotis in a curve, creating a smooth mediation between the front of the building with its surroundings. The vertical mass, cutting into the hillside, takes on the form of a straight-lined bar, standing tall and majestically against the valley. Where these two masses meet lies a transparent lobby space.

The main lobby area is on the upper floor level where multiple pedestrian access is possible
One access is made from level one of the facility east of the back building where a wooder
walkway extends from the main entrance out into the greenery. The other access to the main
entrance is by walking on a series of granite steps to an intimate courtyard where visitors
are drawn and led to an entrance canopy viewed from all sides.

The dwelling units are organized in a series of rows, each following the respective profile of the front and back buildings. Each unit is organized in such a way that all units have scenic views of the surrounding mountains.

The main lobby between the two buildings is all glazed to maximize transparency and illuminate the common areas where visitors lounge, exercise, and dine. To further enhance the interconnection between the two buildings, a catwalk links an outdoor deck in the back of the building, an extension of the dining area, to an open terrace in the front, which serves as

an outlook point onto the courtyard and the fan-shaped row of units visible behind the double glazing. An indoor linear stair, organizing the circulation pattern in the common area, acts as a stage in the main atrium space. The sloping nature of the site allows for a multi-level access and makes the journey to and from nature seamless.

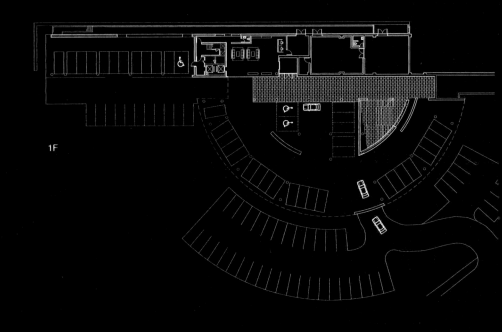

1F

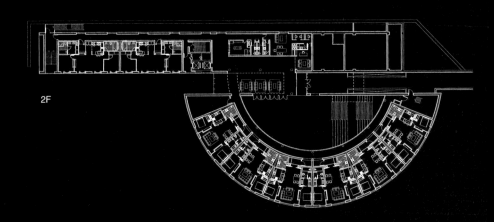

2F

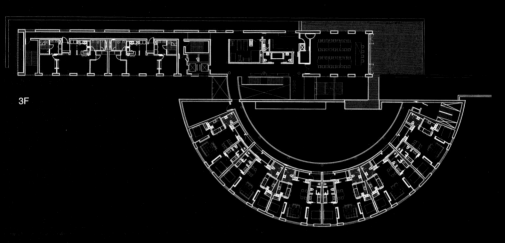

3F

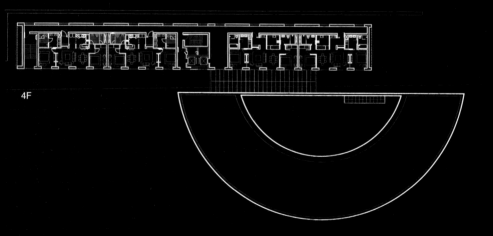

4F

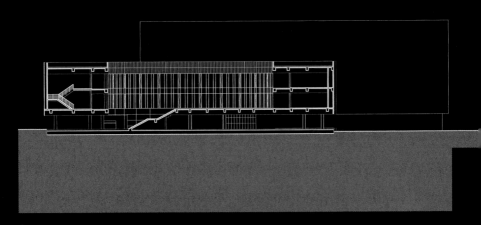

Section

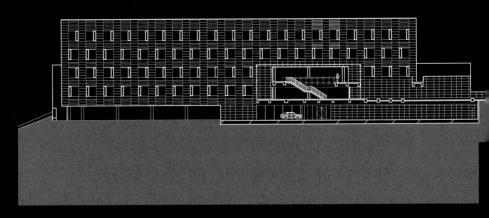

Elevation

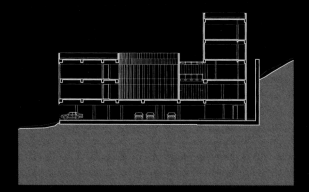

Section

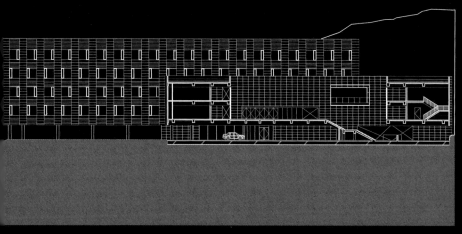

Elevation

RFB HOUSE

RFB HOUSE

California, USA, 2009

The site located on a steep hill offers no choice but to excavate to create an entry. A vertical stacking of spaces, connected by an elevator and stair core, create variations in plans, sections, and elevations. Dynamic yet organic movement of tree trunks and the leaf patterns of Eucalyptus trees on site offered inspirations for overall compositions and elevations.

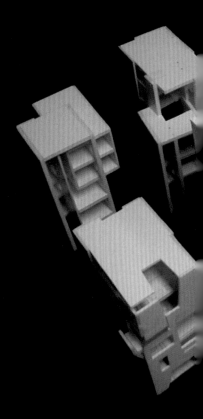

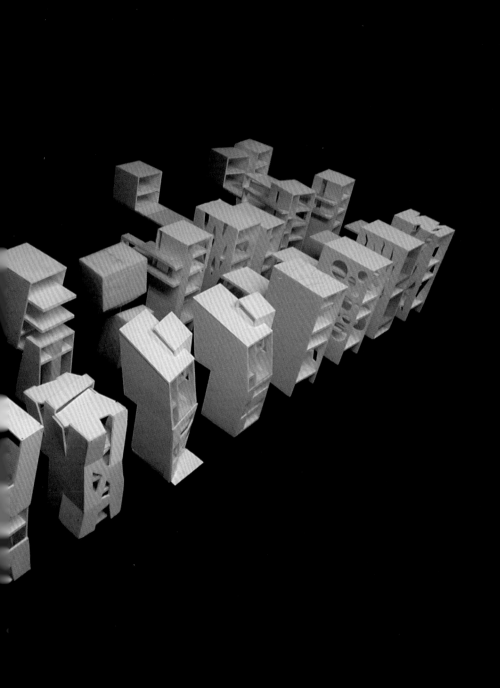

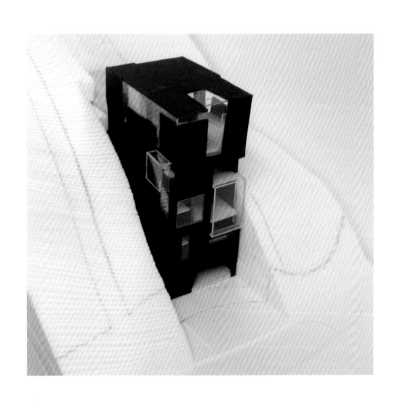

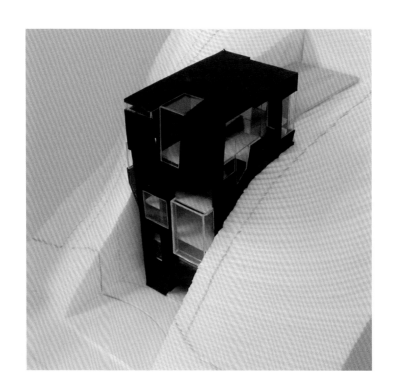

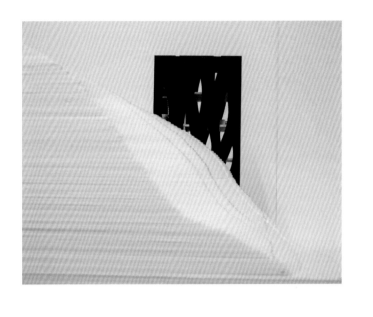

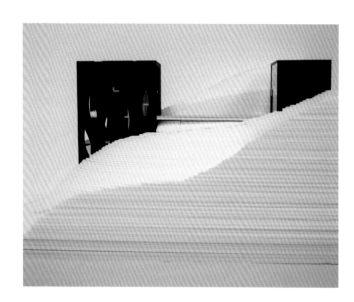

YANGPYEONG HOUSE

YANGPYEONG HOUSE

Yangpyeong-gun, Gyeonggi-do, 2007

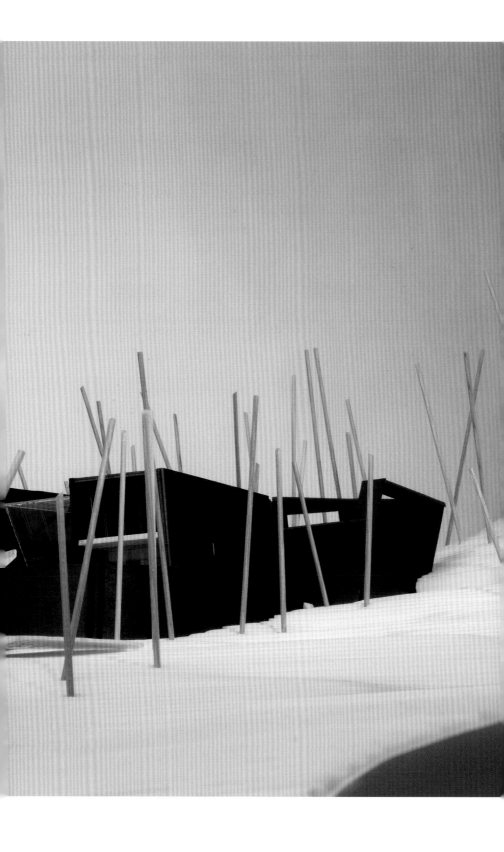

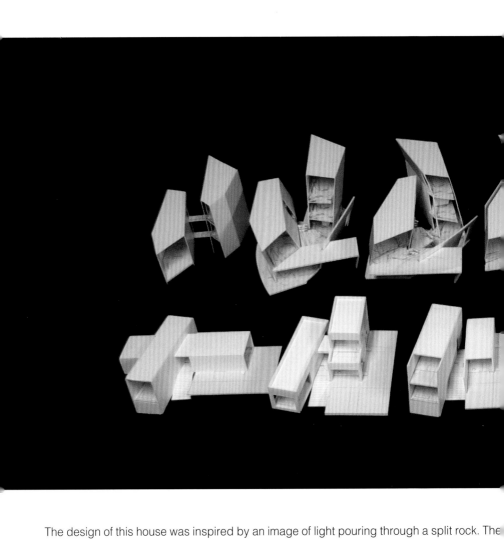

The design of this house was inspired by an image of light pouring through a split rock. The site is located on a wooded hill which offers panoramic views of the mountains beyond. Taking advantage of the site, the dynamic design accommodates the various needs of the family.

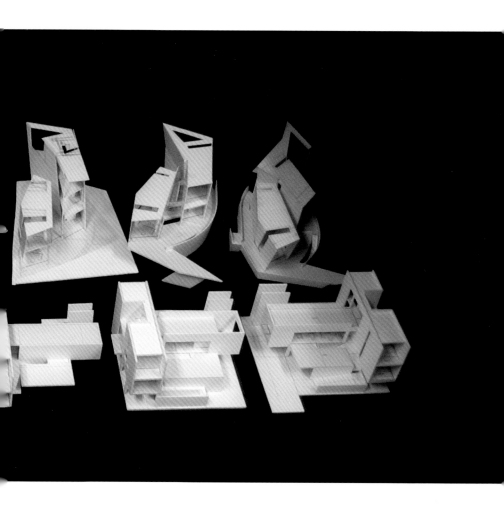

members. Hence, Yangpyeong House is not only a reaction to the natural setting of the forest but also an emotional manifestation inspired by the site.

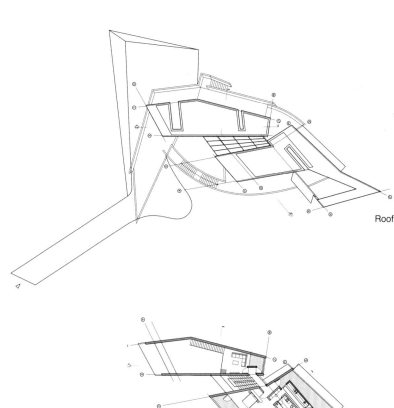

Roof

2F

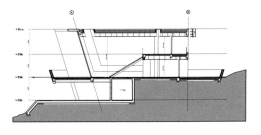

Section

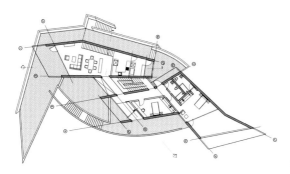

1F

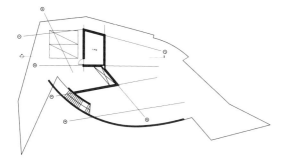

B1

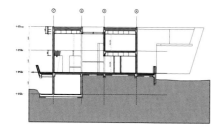

Section

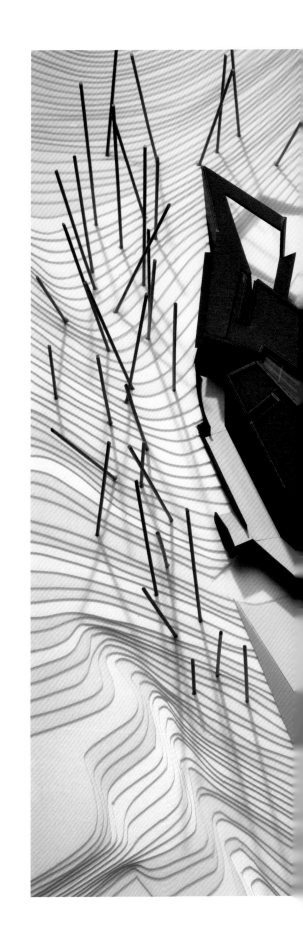

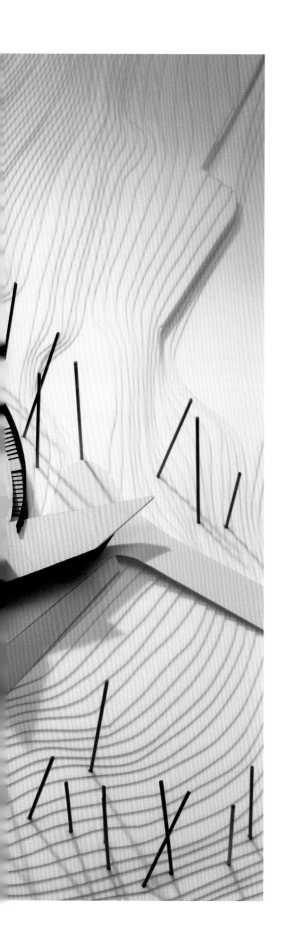

YONGIN HOUSE

YONGIN HOUSE

Yongin-si, Gyeonggi-do, 2006

In the foreground of the residence, spectacular foothills of the mountain unfold. The design concept was to integrate architecture with nature which is exemplified in the spatial sequence as one enters the house. The main access to the residence is via a stairway that starts from the side of the basement level and passes to the forecourt

(*madang*) via a small courtyard. All the rooms, including
the living room, dining room, kitchen, and the bedrooms
are open to the exterior view. The rooms are linked by
a glazed corridor.

Exposed concrete, the main construction material, was used to articulate the expressive form. To reinforce the concept of "openness" and connection with nature, the exterior enclosure is mostly transparent. Moving along the interior hall, one experiences the blurring of inside and outside.

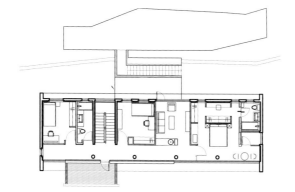

2F

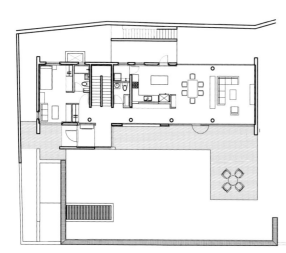

1F

B1

JOAN-RI HOUSE

JOAN-RI HOUSE

Namyangju-si, Gyeonggi-do, 2005

In an open field, the elongated composition of Joan-ri House captures the spirit of the expansive site. In Joan-ri House, the rectilinear walls and horizontal members are intentionally composed to frame the landscape in such a way where architecture and landscape are merged to create a holistic design.

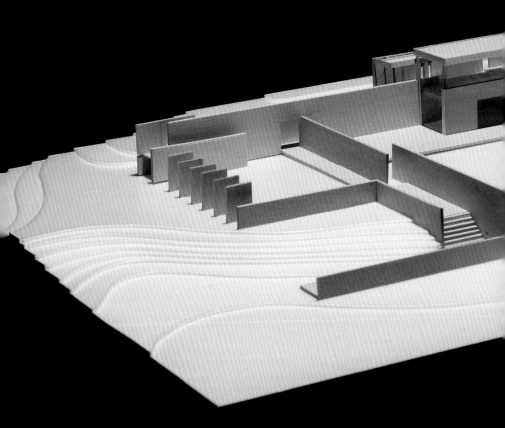

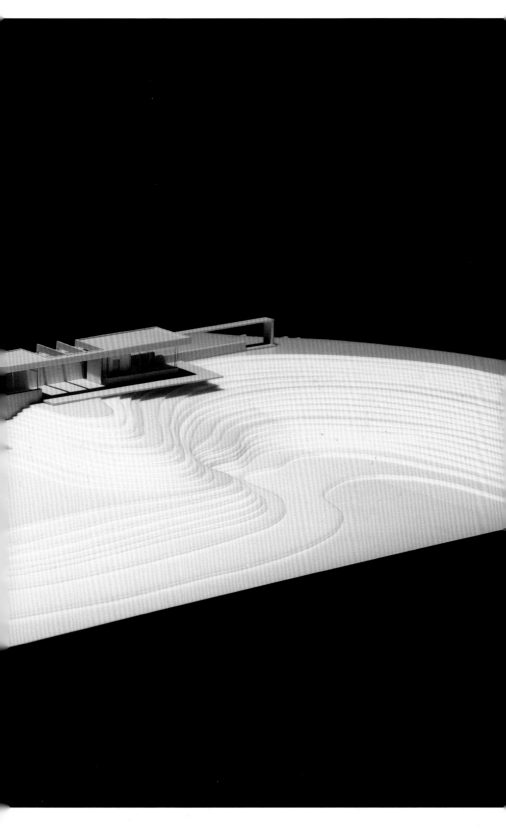

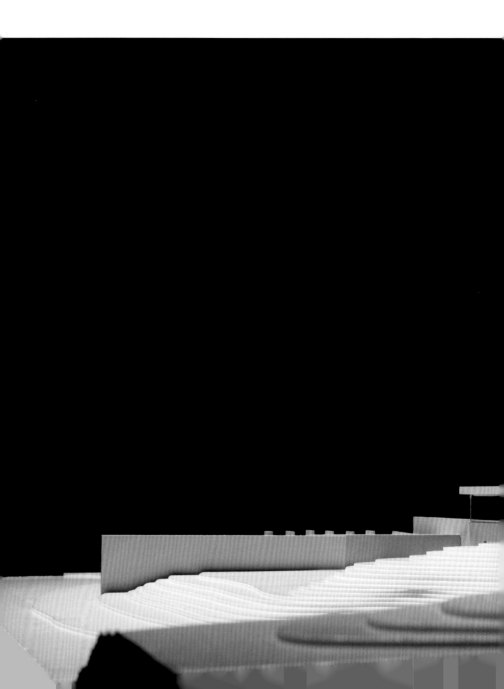

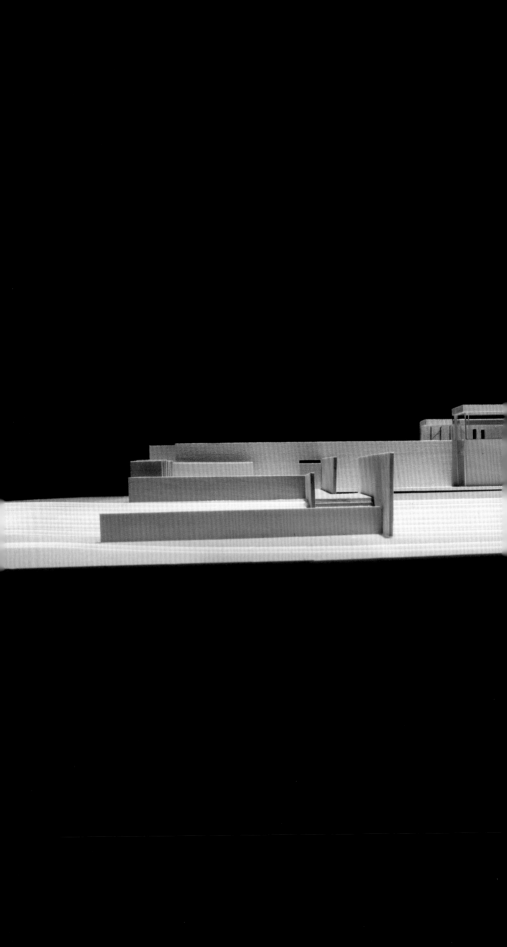

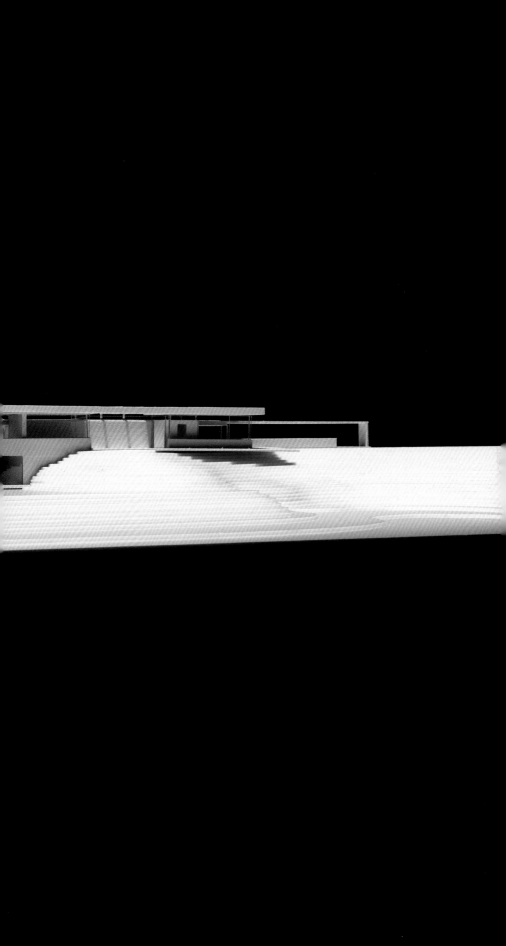

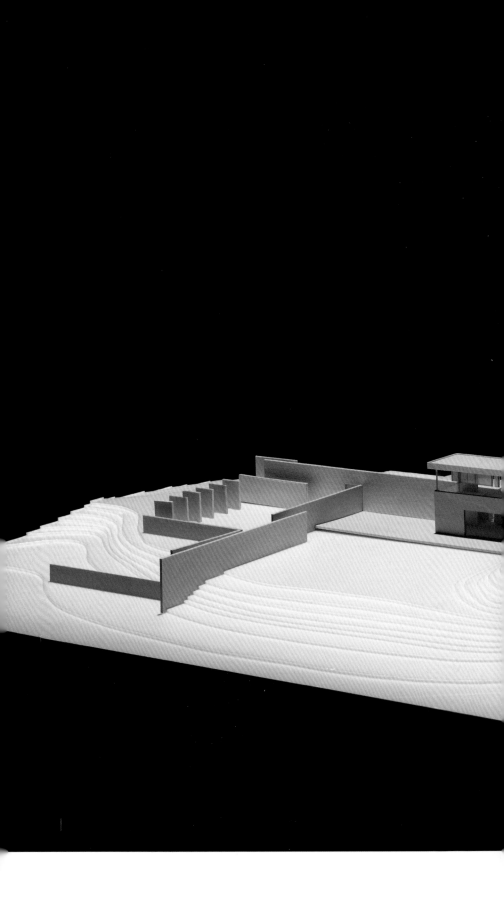

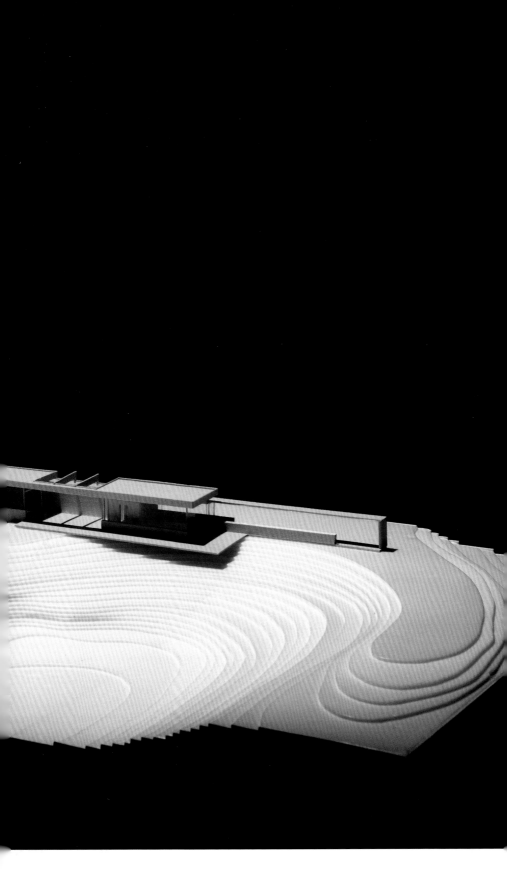

GLASS HOUSE

GLASS HOUSE

Gwangju-si, Gyeonggi-do, 2002

In the outskirts of Seoul, the Glass House is located in a rural community at the foot of the hill facing a small river. Some main design issues to consider were scale, form, and overall flow of the site. Furthermore, the design had to meet the client's request for a reading room and an informal space to have tea and discussions. The Glass House at the end of the hill is the central figure surrounded by nature with limitless views. The design highlights the house as an object, standing boldly midst of nature. Walls define the boundary of utilitarian programs while the use of glass clearly distinguish the closed space from the open space. Entering the transparent hall and following the curved wall, one experiences the contrast of closed and open space with limited views before reaching the main space that opens up to the outside.

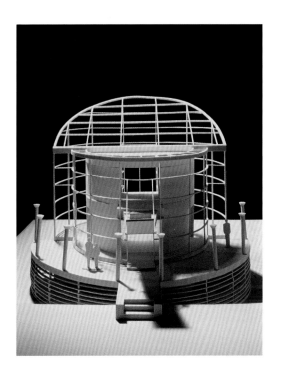

YEONHEE-DONG HOUSE

YEONHEE-DONG HOUSE

Yeonhee-dong, Seoul, 2001

This residence project brought to fore the relational question between the traditional courtyard and the building that is to occupy a site that looks onto a regular residential street. The first thing that was striking when visiting the site upon the design request was the fact that the existing building and the inner courtyard bore no relationship whatsoever. The house had to be rebuilt from ground up and at the core of the design problem was to re-address the relationship of the building as it relates to the site. The program of this house was for the residence of a couple of advanced age, one adult grown-up child and two other children that were under the couple's supervision. It also was a place for occasional sleep-ins for children who are no longer part of the regular household. Ample space for sleeping and storage was necessary as well.

As for the building layout, a two-story living room takes the main stage of the building. At the ground level an annex study room that connects to the master bedroom is brought out to the foreground facing the inner courtyard. The intent was to actively engage the inner courtyard to the rest of the building and create a harmonious relationship between the interior and the exterior of the building.

ITAEWON HOUSE

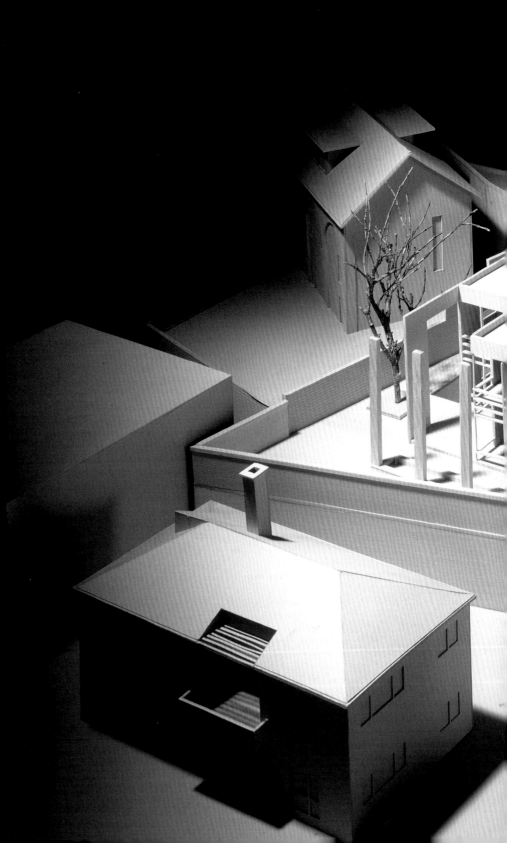

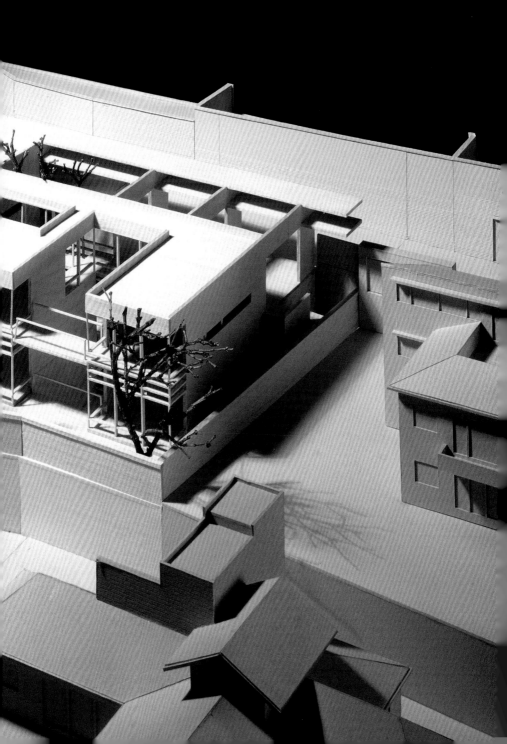

ITAEWON HOUSE

Itaewon-dong, Seoul, 2001

An outdoor entry courtyard, a key design element of the Itaewon House, was a solution to
accommodate the extreme site topography. The plan of the house revolves around two in

ernal courtyards in order to provide ample light and privacy. The minimal street façade vith the light-filled entry courtyard acts as a datum for the entire circulation sequence.

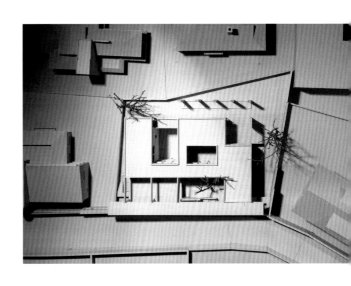

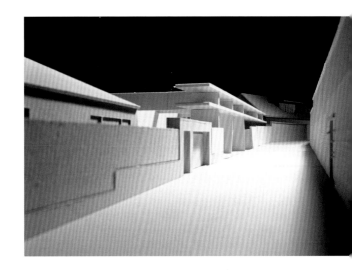

LEE HOUSE

LEE HOUSE

Seongnam-si, Gyeonggi-do, 1998

In designing the Lee House, the relationship between the house, outside, and the site was the main consideration. Nestled in the mountainside, the house is sensitively integrated with nature, and the boundary between inside and outside is blurred. The house is situated to maximize the view and garden area. In approaching the house, one meanders to the entry while experiencing the striking relationship between the building and the nature.

SEOCHO-DONG HOUSE

SEOCHO-DONG HOUSE

Seocho-dong, Seoul, 1992

The site slated for the construction of the house was no longer a vacant lot. Except for the soaring sky above and the sun beyond, visual noise from the surroundings were crowding in on the cramped space. Before filling this void, the site had to be neutralized with a sound of silence. The design of the house itself had to be timeless so that foreshadowing of the future was as palpable and real as modern life and the longing for things past. The house had to be thoroughly imbued with a restrained elegance which is intensified with the passage of time.

The use of strong contrast between shadow and light and juxtaposition of closed and open spaces along the narrow exterior corridor heightens the drama of earth dropping away from under you and the uplifting sky above. Rarely does one experience such dramatic tension between two elemental forces of nature at work in an urban residential setting. The desire for this awakening of senses may have stemmed from the urban dweller's yearning for deeper experiences in his daily life.

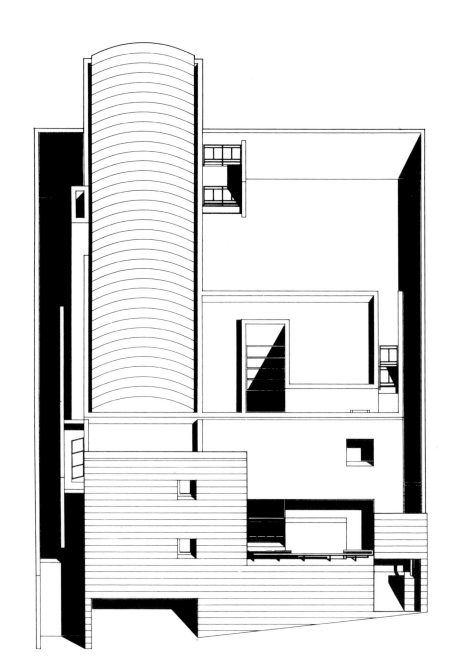

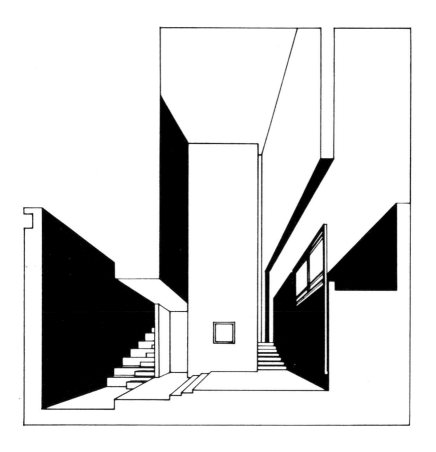

JEJU-DO HOUSE

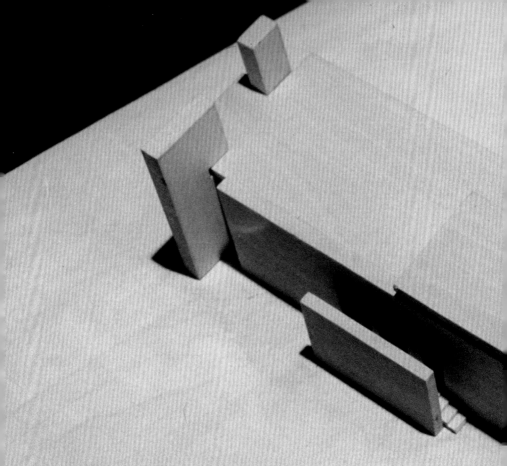

JEJU-DO HOUSE

Jeju-do, 1987

The site commands a striking view from its dramatic promontory. It juts out into
an open sea and is surrounded on three sides by the water. In the back, one
can see far off in the distance the peak of Mount Halla. The owner requested a
Western style weekend house. The exposed nature of the site required that the
building be firmly anchored to the ground with minimum of exposure to the harsh
elements of the island. And yet the protection from the elements had to be read
as a gesture of confident bracing, not of shy retreat, for something in this rocky
and windy island stirs one's instinct to be closer to the earth.

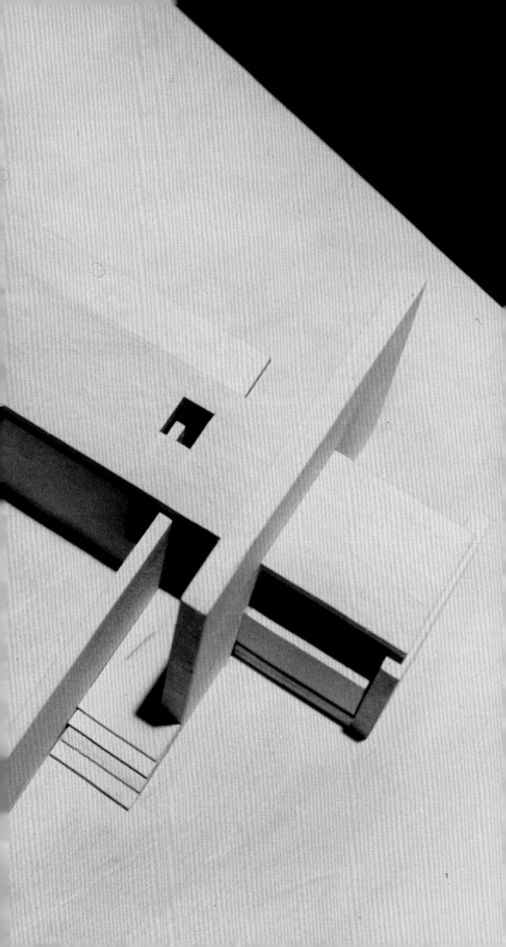

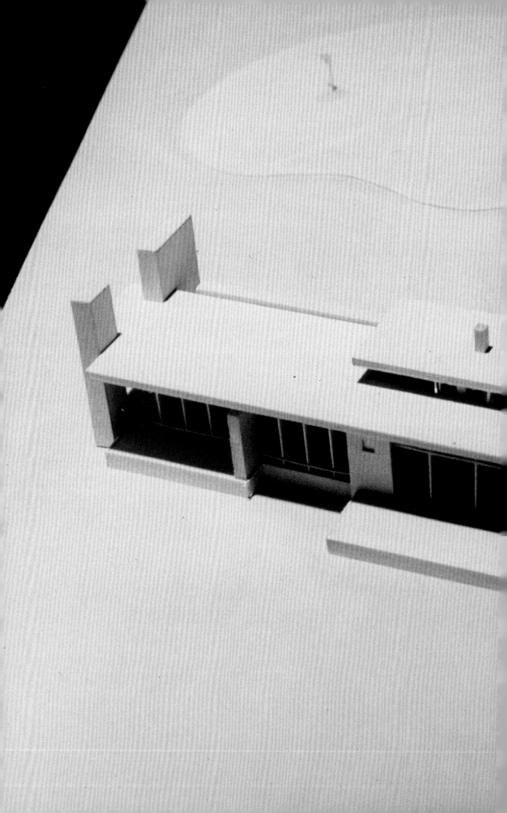

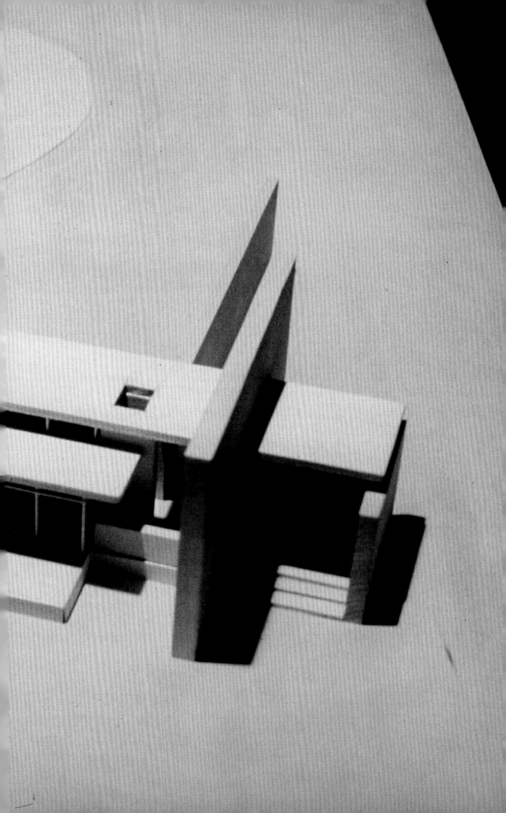

JOIL BUILDING

JOIL BUILDING

Nonhyeon-dong, Seoul, 2004

Located in a quiet inner city block, the site was seemingly more conducive for either residential or neighborhood-friendly facilities rather than an office building. In order to accommodate commercial as well as office programs, an attempt was made to break away from the typical notion of "core and shell," which is usually found in building layouts, by splitting the entrance area into two venues; one leading to a restaurant on the first floor and the other leading to the main core of the office spaces on the upper floors. This separation is expressed with the circulation core exposed to the streets, giving a sense of delineation between the commercial space and the office space. The front curtain wall façade acts as a transparent box encasing the main volume of the building, thereby evoking an image of "a building within a building."

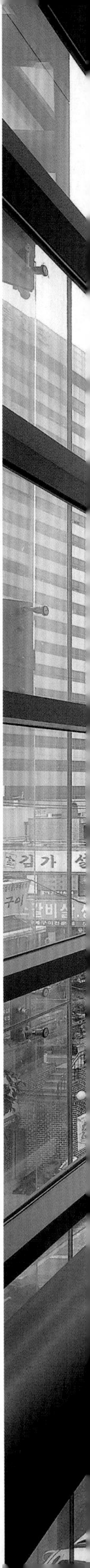
김 가

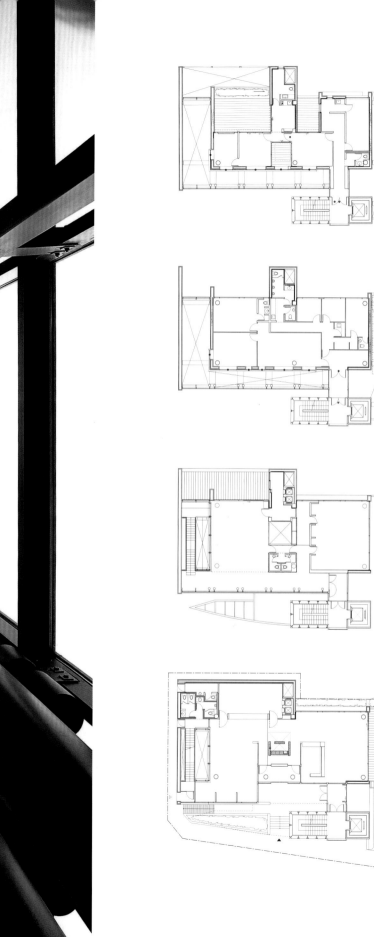

4F

3F

2F

1F

MAYA BUILDING

MAYA BUILDING

Paju-si, Gyeonggi-do, 2004

The site is located on a wedge-shaped lot at the backside of the Paju Bookcity. The building design was approached with an understanding that office and storage spaces would share the same level of importance in terms of hierarchy. The identity and relation between those spaces that would accommodate the two distinct programs became an important issue to address. An attempt was made to use different building forms and materials in order to reflect the given conditions.

The original design intention was to establish the idea of two sub-buildings that would share the same characteristics based on the schematic design. With respect to spatial organization, the two masses are separated on the first floor where the main entrance is located and reconnected on the second floor to provide spatial efficiency and architectural clarity. The connection between the two masses is made by a bridge on the second floor.

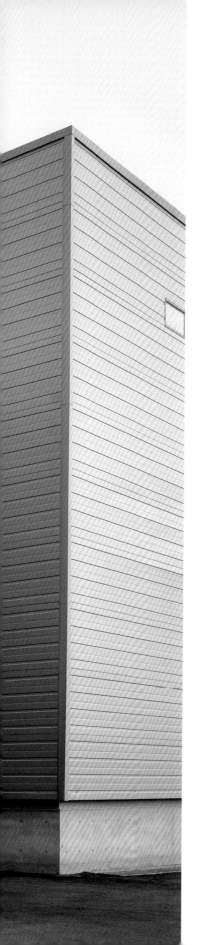

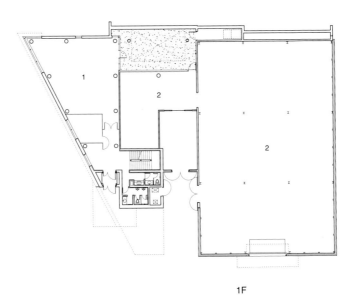

1F
1. Office
2. Storage

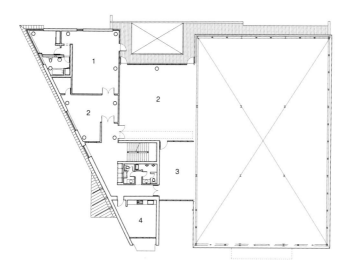

2F
1. President's room
2. Office
3. Conference room
4. Dining room

YEONGCHANG PRINTING

YEONGCHANG PRINTING

Paju-si, Gyeonggi-do, 2005

Designing a factory can be a challenge for architects because of the functional requirement often imposed by the program, which leaves very little room for creativity.

In the case of Yeongchang Printing, building materials such as aluminum panels, etched glasses and bright colors were used to express industrial aesthetics. The articulation of the building on the street side was an attempt to express its sculptural presence to the street. Diffused natural light through etched glass windows serves as the primary light source inside the factory.

SAMPYO BUILDING

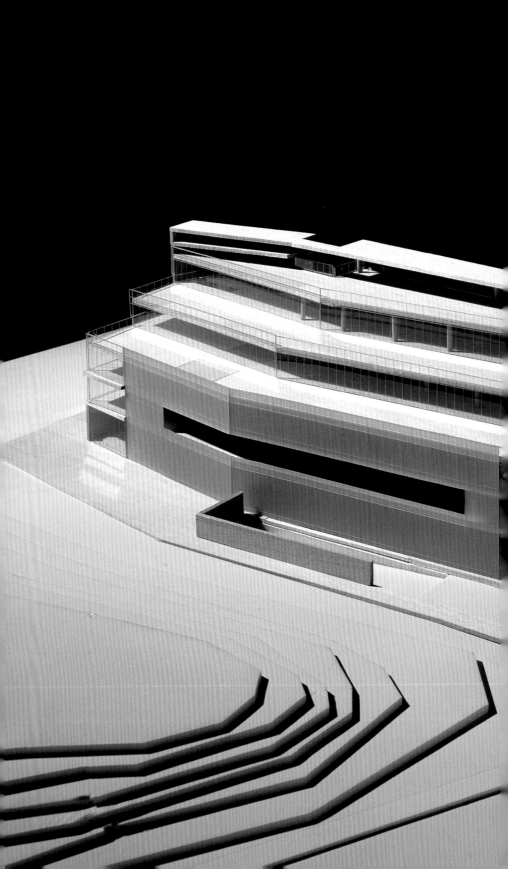

SAMPYO BUILDING

Pungnap-dong, Seoul, 2001

This project represents an architect's attempt to enliven the nexus between individuality and collectivity within the context of architecture in the coming decade. Conceived as a new brand of multi-functional building that embraces the diverse needs for cultural, institutional and commercial expression, the building meets a specific set of demands imposed by the historical site itself while striving to express the individuality of the users. It does so by capturing the common vision of the site and the building and casting it in the spirit of the forthcoming decade. Located next to the eastern berm built in the Baek-jae period (approximately 300 A.D.) to serve as a defensive wall, the design had to meet stringent height restrictions.

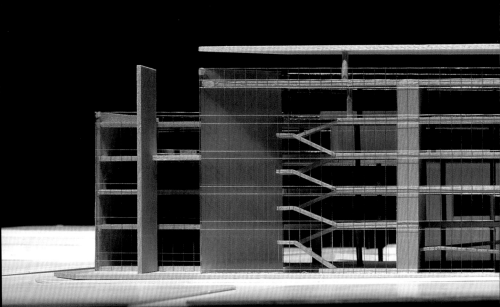

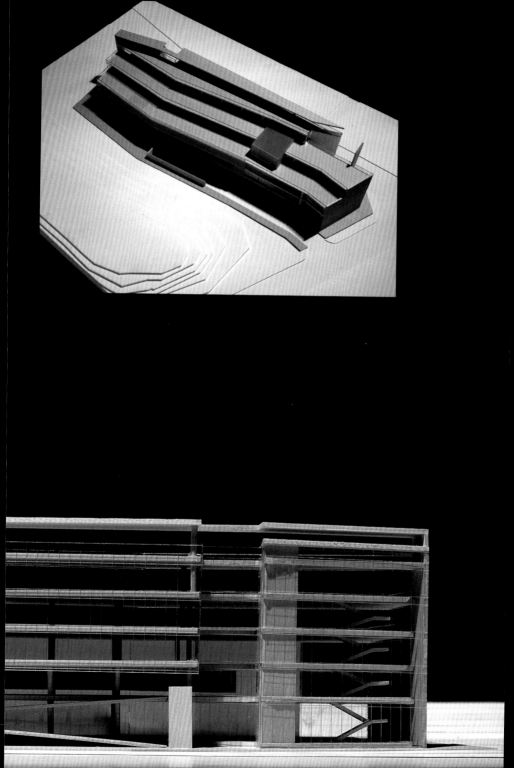

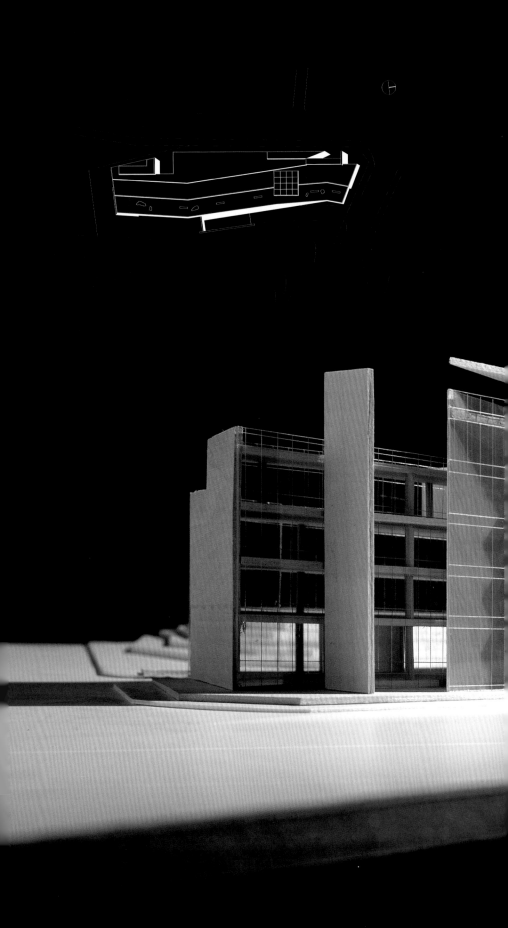

The building volume cascades down towards the earthen berm partially to accommodate the restriction of building height imposed by the historical commission. The design of the building invites the occupants and visitors to appreciate the architectural dynamism between two man-made structures found over the time span of three millennia and exhibits fully its architectural freedom by setting the stage for its users to experience what the building offers.

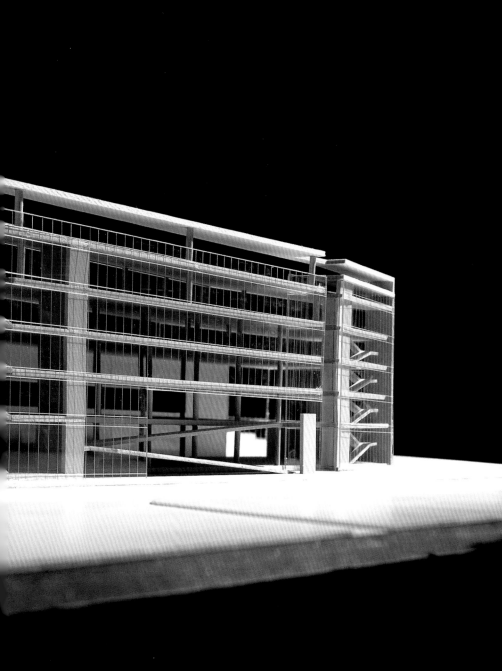

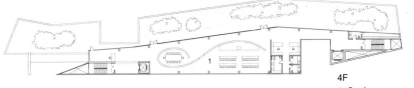

4F
1. Conference room

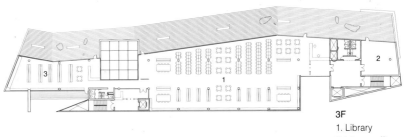

3F
1. Library
2. Library office
3. Stack room

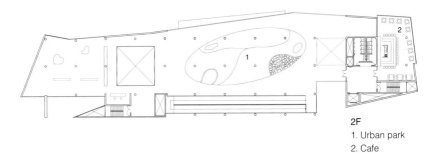

2F
1. Urban park
2. Cafe

1F
1. Bookstore
2. Record store
3. Restaurant
4. Hi-tech showroom

NEW KOREA COUNTRY CLUB

NEW KOREA COUNTRY CLUB
RENOVATION

Goyang-si, Gyeonggi-do, 2006

The club house that was built in the 1970s was in desperate need of renovation of the interior spaces. Design details and materials were used in moderation lest they create too much contrast with the dated, original exposed concrete exterior. Renovation includes reception, lounge, main dining hall, private dining rooms and locker rooms.

NAMSAN BUILDING

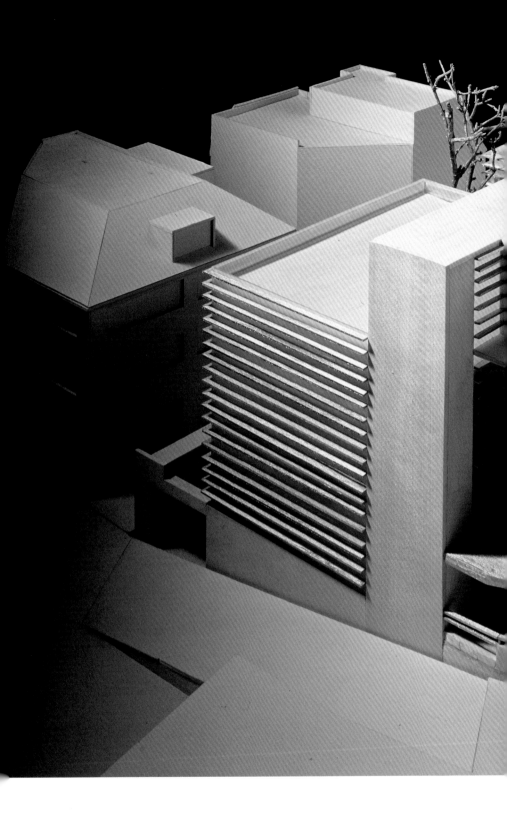

NAMSAN BUILDING

Namsan-dong, Seoul, 2000

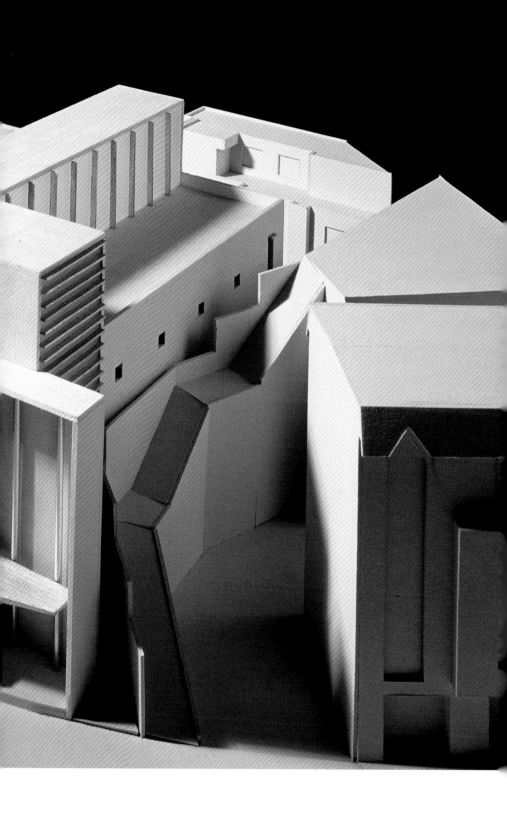

The project site is located in a commercial district between the lower part of Namsan Freeway and Myeong-dong. The building, which is to be used as a fashion design office, was envisioned to provoke a fashionable lifestyle and highlight the contrast with the dated buildings in the neighborhood. As for the building materials, limestone was proposed to be used for the rear face of the building whereas glass was used as the transparent skin on the three frontal faces of the building.

WEDGE

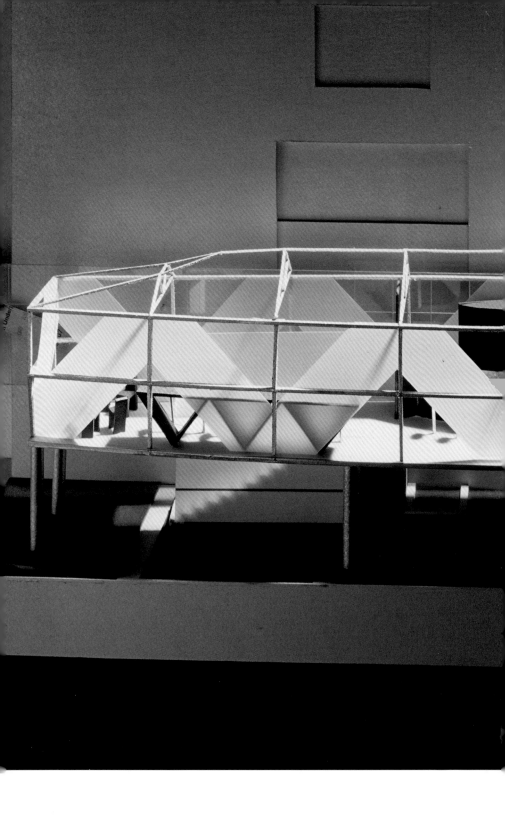

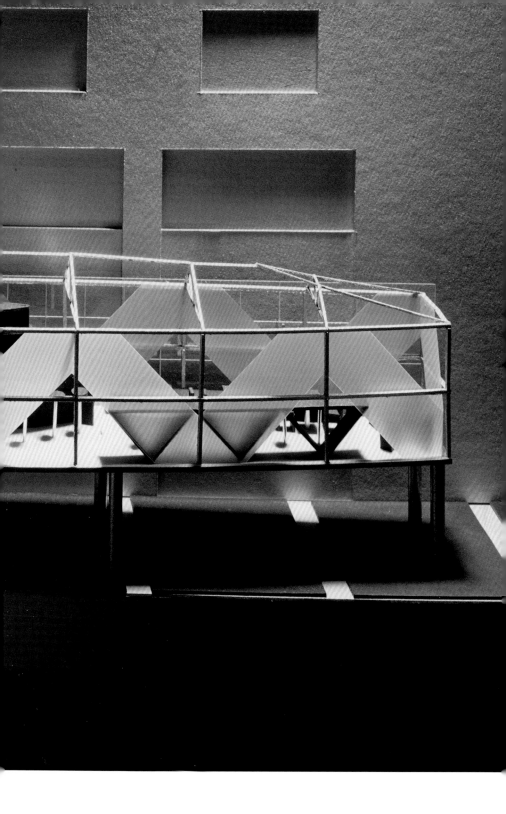

WEDGE

Samseong-dong, Seoul, 2000

The site for this project is a leeway space docked between two high-rise buildings in one of the busiest commercial areas in Seoul. An attempt was made to use the building — a wine bar — as a connector between the main road in the front and the service road in the back within the urban context. The building is on a piloti and bold graphic pattern was used on the glass to reflect the dynamic energy of downtown Seoul.

YOUNG PROJECT

YOUNG PROJECT

Yeoksam-dong, Seoul, 2008

Diverse design solutions were explored for a four-story
building located in the corner of an urban block in Seoul.
Variations in massing and building materials were inves-
tigated and proposed.

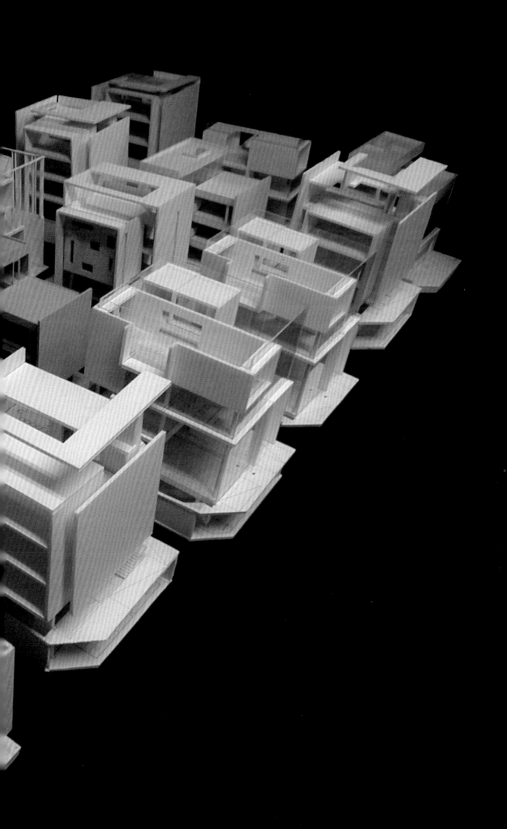

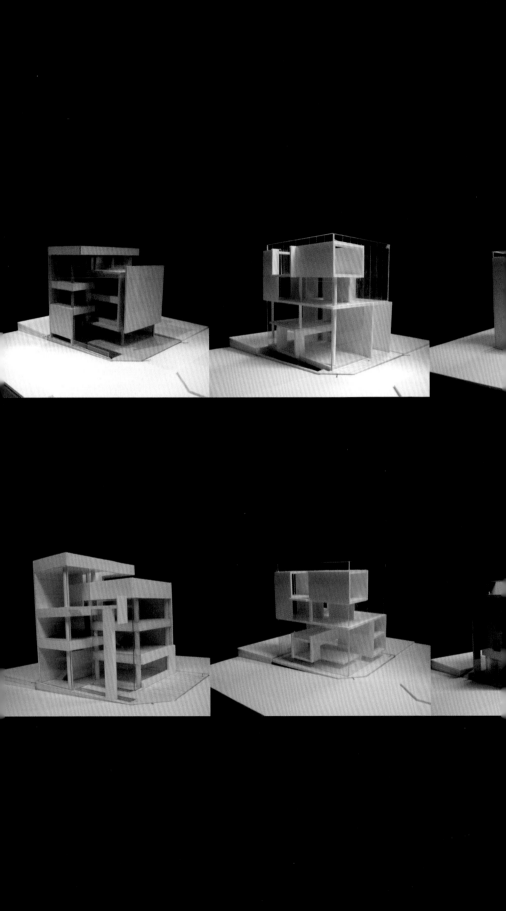

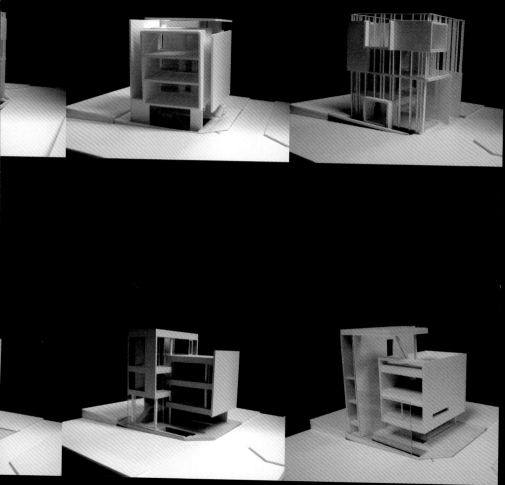

CHOI'S HARDWARE COMPANY

CHOI'S HARDWARE COMPANY

Nonhyeon-dong, Seoul, 1997

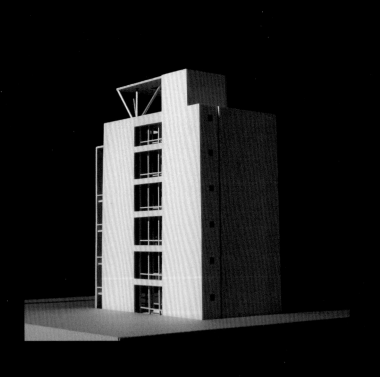

The site had conditions typical to its city location one block away from a busy intersection in the southern part of the Han River (Gangnam). Existing buildings flanked the site on either sides and the narrow frontage was toward a busy street. The building was to be used as an office headquarter for a hardware company that deals in architectural hardware. Considering the site conditions and the program, an atrium was put in the center of the building as a focal point to bring in light and to mark the main circulation zone. The design of this building seeks to express not only the hard materiality of the wares being sold but also the perceptive sensitivity of the people who handle the seemingly hard but exacting objects.

SHANGHAI INTL. CENTER

SHANGHAI
INTERNATIONAL CENTER

Shanghai, China, 1997
Associate Architect: Samwoo Architects

The client for the invited architectural design competition sought an innovative design appropriate for the international commercial center in Shanghai. The site was situated in a prominent location in the city which covered almost an entire city block. The proposed design called for all the required programs to be vertically separated in one building mass which was to contain all the required facilities.

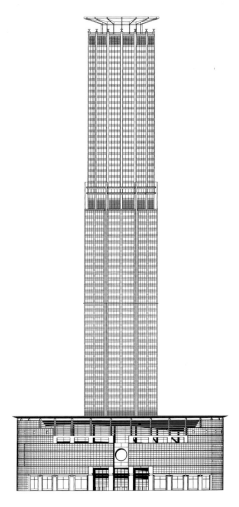

Front elevation

Spaces for the office and the hotel were located in the tower in ascending order and high-end shopping malls were located in the lower part of the cylindrical building. The atrium space where the tower meets the lower part of the building connects the two while serving as a convenient and pleasant shopping arcade with plenty of natural light.

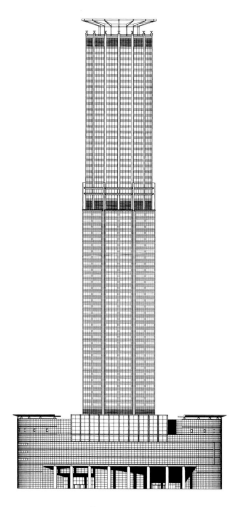

Rear elevation

SAEGANG BUILDING

SAEGANG BUILDING

Yeoksam-dong, Seoul, 1990

The site overlooks a royal tomb full of pine trees whose aroma permeates the site amid the tranquil serenity. The building has to be a visual manifestation of the tamed urban vitality harnessed through the fusion between the silence of the dead and the chaotic energy of the living. In plan, the core was located in the rear of the building in order to maximize the view to the park, and in the process ample space for the entry lobby was secured. The front façade was of curtain wall with a curved plane that enables the maximum exposure to the greenery, and the presence of the royal tomb was acknowledged by the large square opening in the center of the building to seek a mode of connection between the past and the present.

GALLERY SAMTUH

GALLERY SAMTUH

Cheongdam-dong, Seoul, 1997

The building functions as an art gallery and a residence. The design intention was to embrace the diverse programs that reflect the owner's lifelong experience of operating an art gallery. The site was located one block from the main thoroughfare in an area lodged between downtown and a residential neighborhood where one must meet the challenge of adapting to the duality of competing scales and images. The site was located at a corner, a situation that brought up the issue of accommodating two different programs in one site without interfering with either's integrity.

In defining the relationship between the building and the site, the design intent was not only to maximize the potential use of the lot but also to design the building in such a way so that the site to be read as a single building block that contains both the solid and the void. Resolving of the building and site relationship in this manner ultimately created an inseparable relationship between the inner space and the outer space, allowing the void space to become just as meaningful a part of the building as the solid space.

In sum, the basic architectural intent was to express the dual characteristics inherent in the site and the functional requirement by separating the line of circulation according to different functional demands.

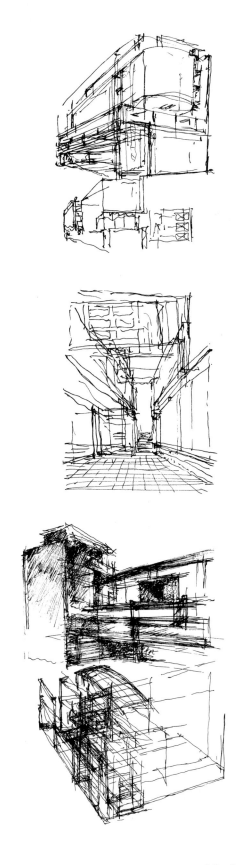

As for the spatial layout, the main entrance to the gallery—located on the second floor—is connected through a bridge that penetrates the void space of the northern side of the building. The parking space is located on the ground floor while the basement is the main exhibition space. For the residential space on the fifth through seventh floors, there are two ways to enter: one is passing through the sized-up balcony of the second floor, and the other is using the stairs and the elevator on the southern side of the building.

All in all, throughout the design process for this building, one of the most significant attempts was to find clarity of space, variety in the spatial experience, and the gravity of the geometric interplay through meditative contemplation and controlled reflection. If this building can find a place in people's memory for a long time to come, it would be enough to inspire an architect to continue his search for that which yet remains unrealized.

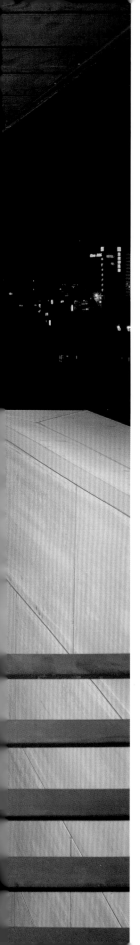

HANGIL ART SPACE 3

HANGIL ART SPACE 3

Paju-si, Gyeonggi-do, 2004

The site is located on top of a sloping hill overlooking the Heyri Art Valley. The main program consists of a house and a gallery. The client requested that the entire complex be designed to be flexible enough to serve multiple functions in the future. Therefore, the building mass as well as its composition needed to be conducive to a harmonious relationship between them.

As such, the dwelling and exhibition spaces were designed to be independent from one another, and yet the outdoor space blurs the boundary between them. The horizontal elongated building mass is placed across the site whereas two other vertical masses are designed to be superimposed on either end of the site, thereby anchoring the building mass firmly to the land. The building design, in the end, becomes a part of nature reflecting the flow of the natural terrain.

GALLERY SEOJONG

GALLERY SEOJONG

Yangpyeong-gun, Gyeonggi-do, 1998

The site, an hour away from the city of Seoul, abuts onto a small stream in front and a hill beyond. The client asked for a space which can be used both as a gallery and a cafe. The basic design intention was to expose the building as much as possible to its natural surroundings and in the process, allow the stream and the hill serve as a main view. Varying the dynamics of the space experienced from both floors of the building, the design sought to bring in the different views of the outside to the inside of the building. In addition, the flying overhang and the canopy over the roof deck were designed to frame the view toward the nature.

A smaller gallery in the original scheme was designed to be built in the front courtyard, and yet only the first phase of the project had been completed. By the time the entire project is completed, the large courtyard and the deck in between will harmoniously complement the surrounding nature.

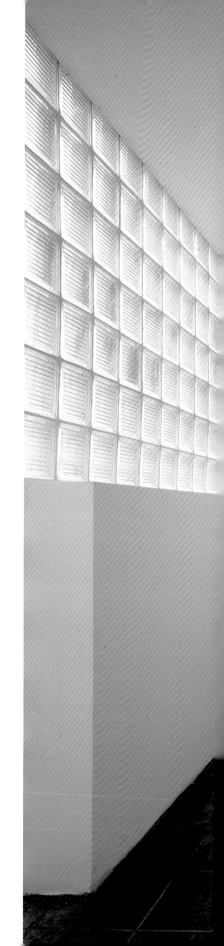

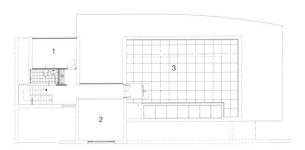

2F
1. Tea room
2. Cafe
3. Roof deck

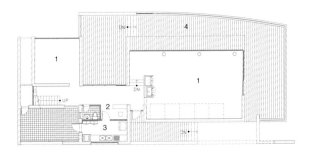

1F
1. Exhibition
2. Reception
3. Kitchen
4. Deck

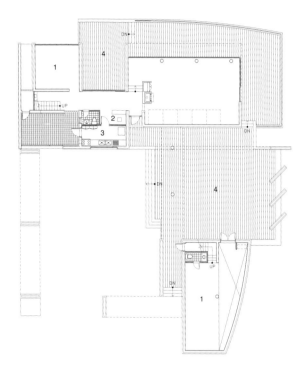

1F of phase 1 & 2
1. Exhibition
2. Reception
3. Kitchen
4. Deck

ART CENTER

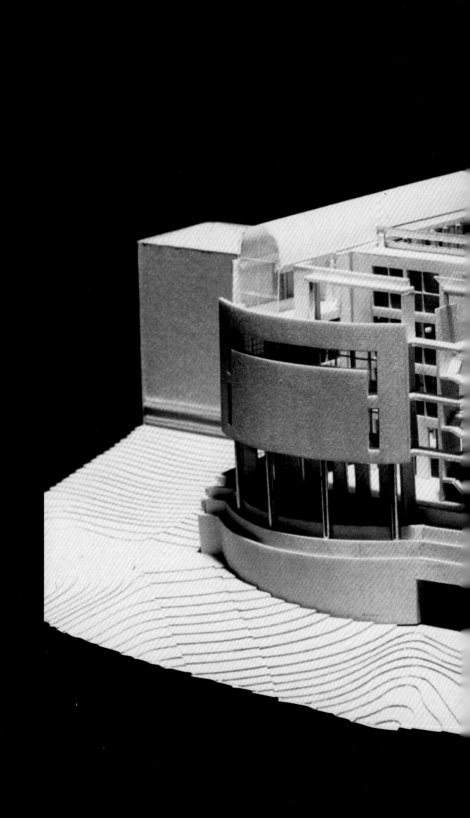

ART CENTER

Yeoksam-dong, Seoul, 1988

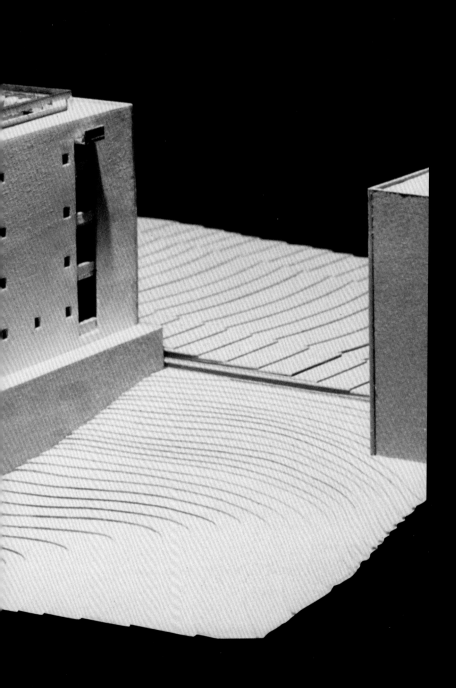

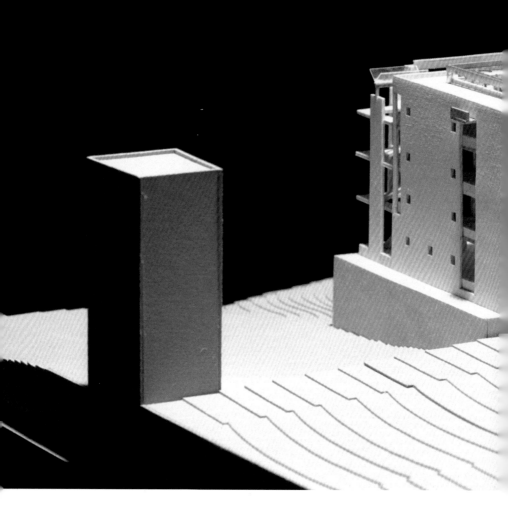

The client is an art collector. Her aspiration is to create an environment where art can be created, displayed and appreciated. The program calls for a gallery space, a studio space for artists and a cafe, a lounge, a conference room and an outdoor space for sculpture, a roof terrace, and parking. The building is as much for the public as it is for the artists. The site is a sloped lot in a newly developing area, the southern part of Han River. In response to the nature of the program and due to the underdeveloped context in which no coherent

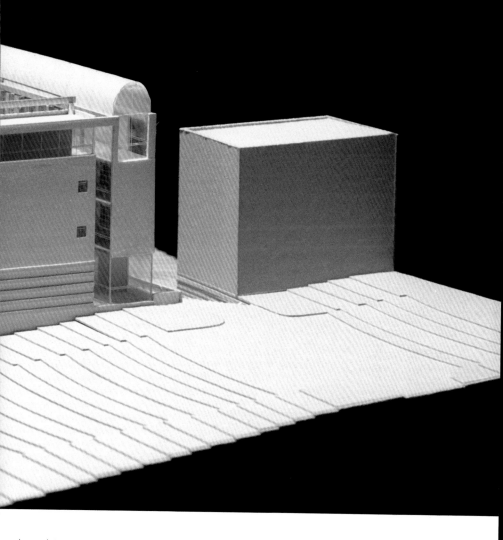

order exists, an attempt was made to create a building that is internally engaging and out-wardly cohesive. To give a strong definition to the site as an urban building block, the build-ing volume is fully stretched out and articulated by two courtyard spaces. The main court acts as a focus where the public can freely linger and appreciate art. Vertical circulations are located diagonally across the main courtyard providing a direct access to the individual studio spaces. The top floor has a walkway that leads to a roof terrace.

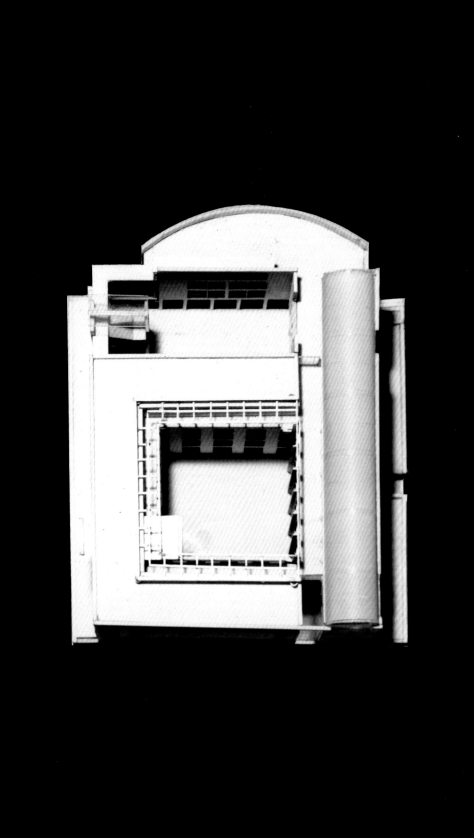

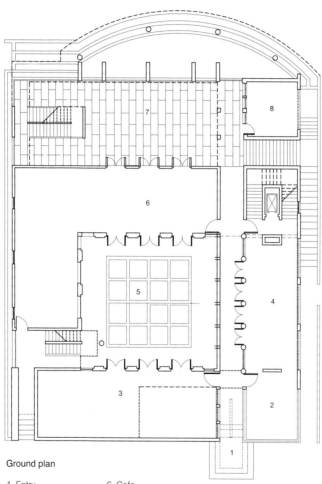

Ground plan

1. Entry
2. Reception
3. Painting gallery
4. Sculpture gallery
5. Court
6. Cafe
7. Sculpture court
8. Service
9. Sunken garden below

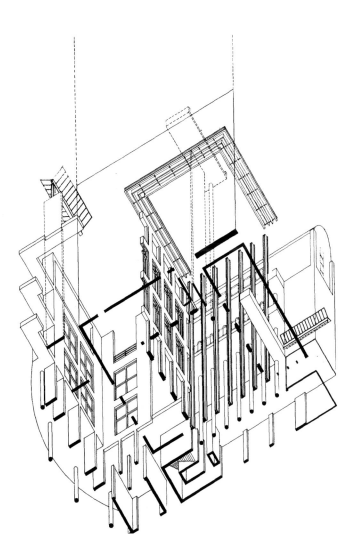

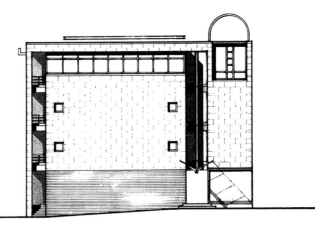

Elevation

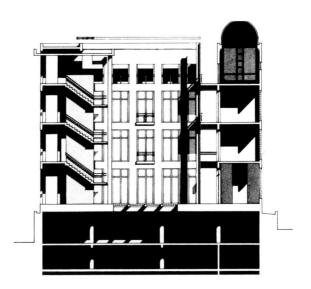

Section

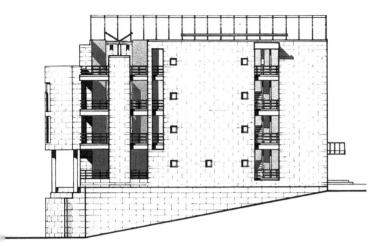

Elevation

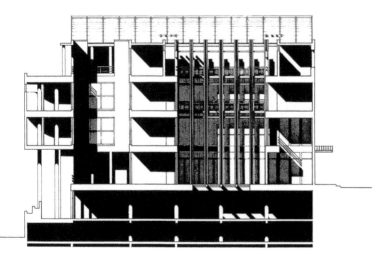

Section

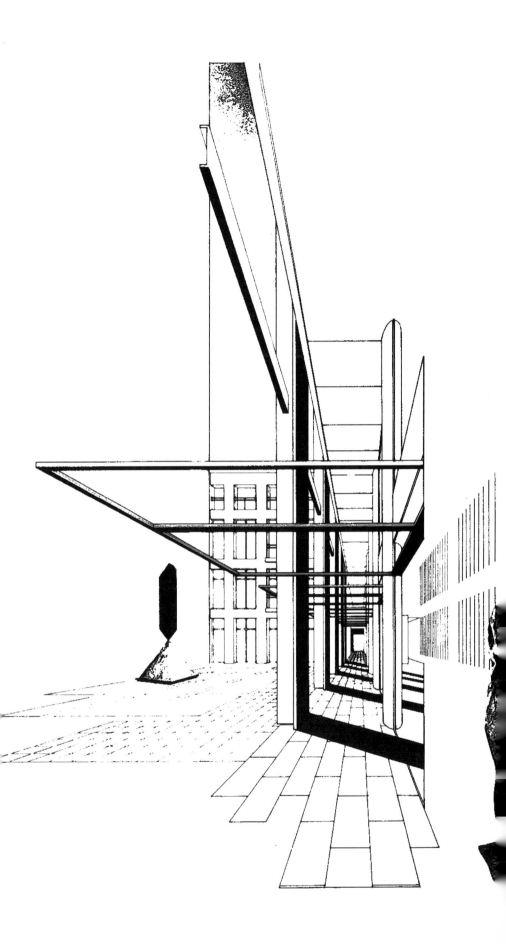

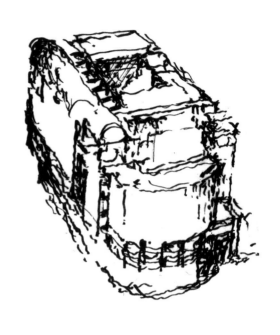

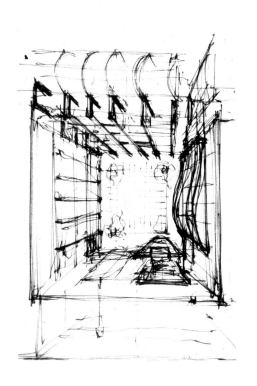

OPEN AIR MUSEUM

OPEN AIR MUSEUM

Euiwang-si, Gyeonggi-do, 1988

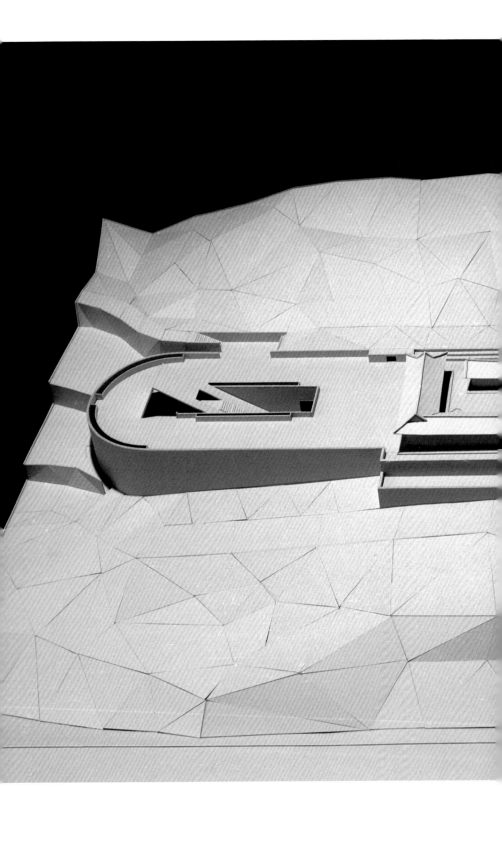

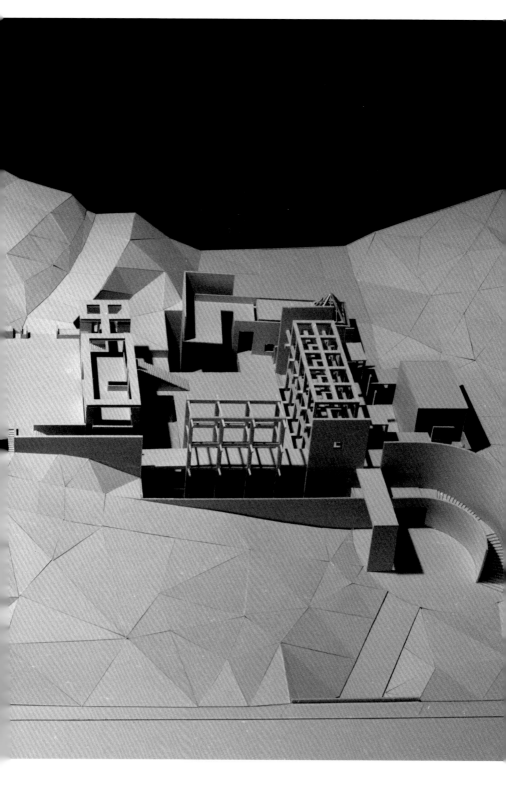

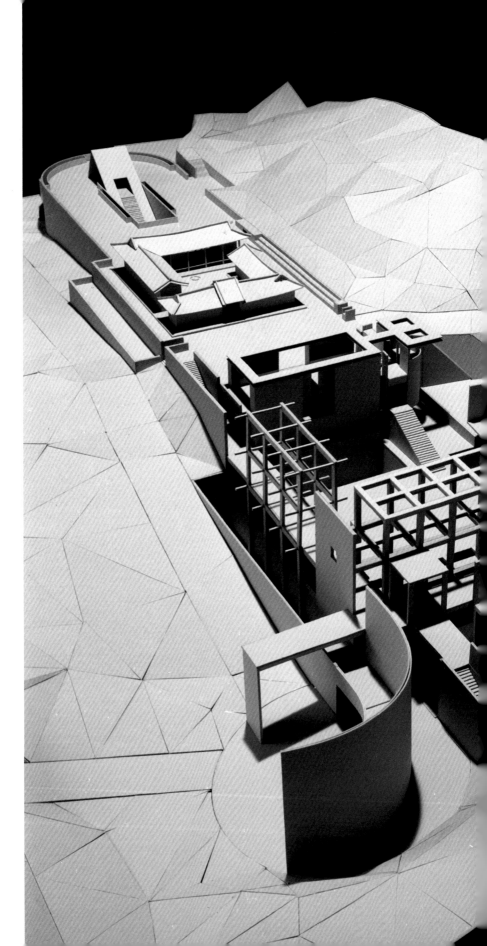

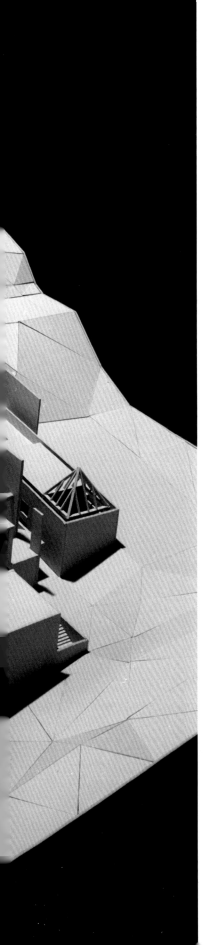

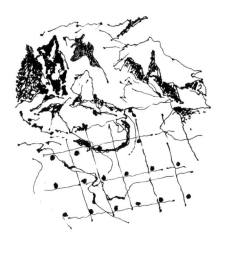

Both in its imposing scale and location, the Main Gallery sets the tone and the scene of the entire museum complex. The Main Gallery marks the beginning of a sequence of the whole built structures on the site. In designing the main gallery, site topography as well as its proximity to the freeway had to come into considerations. Articulation of the building volume vertically in section not only enables the placement of the building mass in harmony with the surrounding topography but also helps to reduce the impression of massiveness as a whole. Also, the distinction of interior and exterior space was diffused wherever possible to awaken and thereby liberate the spirit of the visitors. By intentionally juxtaposing elements of gravity and movement with open, skeletal screens, an introverted composition that itself induces introspection was accomplished.

THE AMPHITHEATER

As an integral part of the outdoor Art Museum, the amphitheater sets a stage as a place for concerts, plays and other performances. The composition for the structures is articulated in such a way that the amphitheater is hidden in the valley instead of being at full exposure to the village nearby. A bridge connects the amphitheater with the cafe and while absorbing energy from all directions, they form a loosely composed mass. This composition, in turn, makes their vertical and horizontal connection possible while eliminating the distracting

forces of untamed nature nearby. The tower came into existence as a result of several considerations; the dynamics of the site as a whole necessitated a vertical focal point. Also, it was necessary to counterbalance the huge electrical transmission towers near the site. Moreover, the tower, which also serves as the bridge's termination point, is a place from which the entire project can be observed. Each end of the almond shaped tower contains an open staircase and a glass elevator.

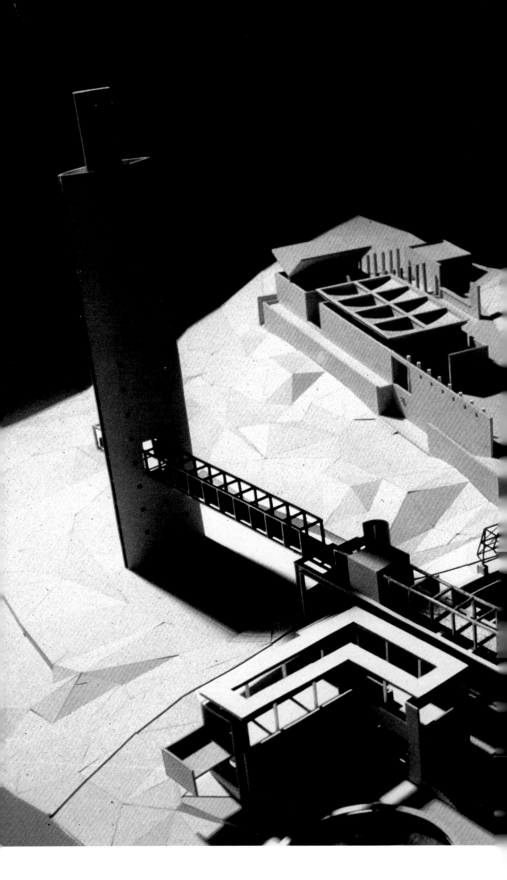

THE GUEST HOUSE

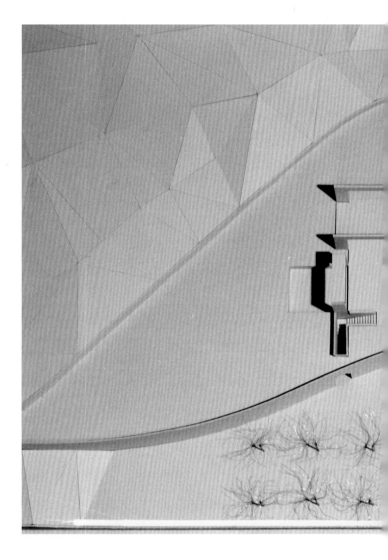

The site for this guest house is located in the eastern edge of the Museum
complex at the foot of the mountain. To establish a sense of place and to
benefit fully from the spectacular view the site commands, a clear yet limited intervention was taken against the given landscape. As a point of
departure, an undulating wall following the topography was proposed to

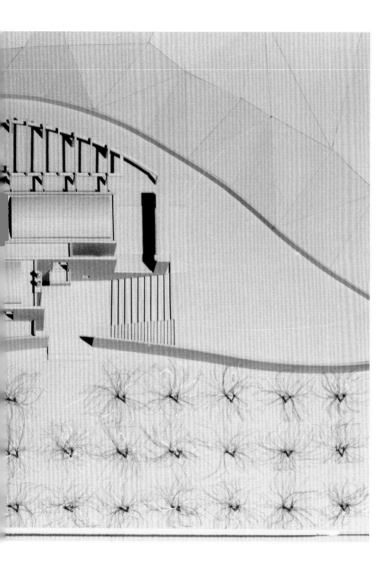

act as a datum against which the house is set and extended out to embrace the landscape. The house itself consists of two split volumes connected by a circulation zone in between to provide each volume with
maximum exposure to the landscape and to ensure privacy at the same
time.

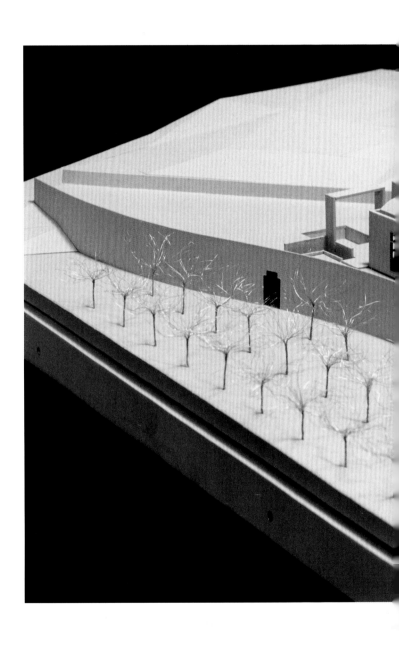

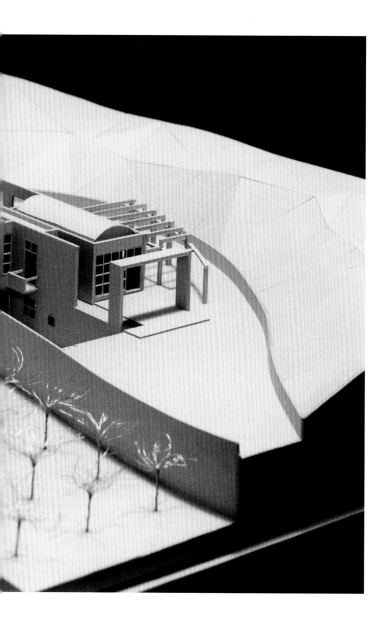

THE RESTAURANT

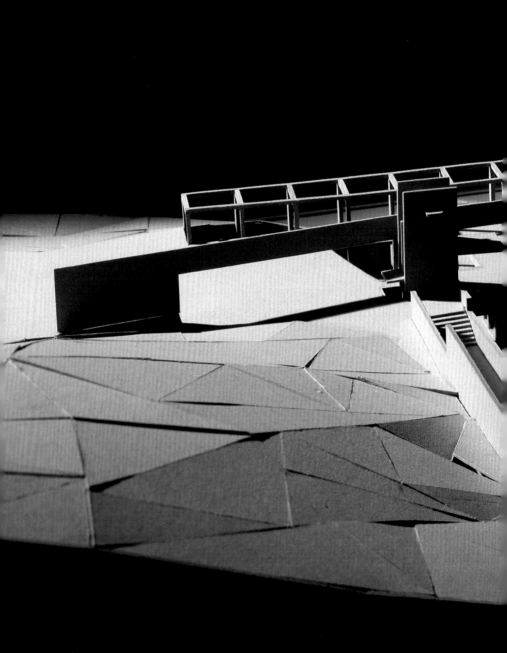

The restaurant scheme reflects the central design concern of making maximum use of the natural geographic composition through a clear delineation of what is natural and built. This harmonious coexistence of the natural and the manmade avoids direct competition with and dominance of one over the other so that the two are allowed to enhance the strength of each other. The scheme takes advantage of the naturally occurring level change to achieve the dynamic approach sequence. The relationship between the two restaurant buildings is that one draws in by compressing the space with intersecting layers of walls and curves while the other building decompresses by releasing the collected energy onto the open space once again. This interplay of the two structures allows the whole surrounding space to participate in the total composition.

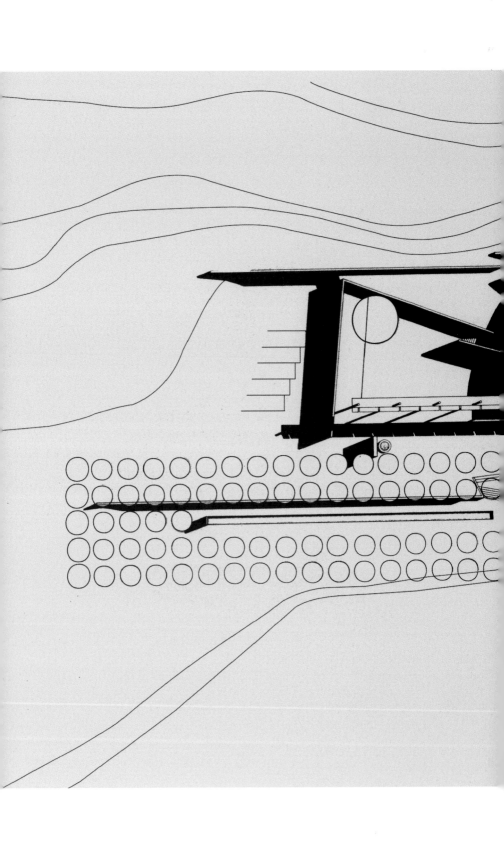

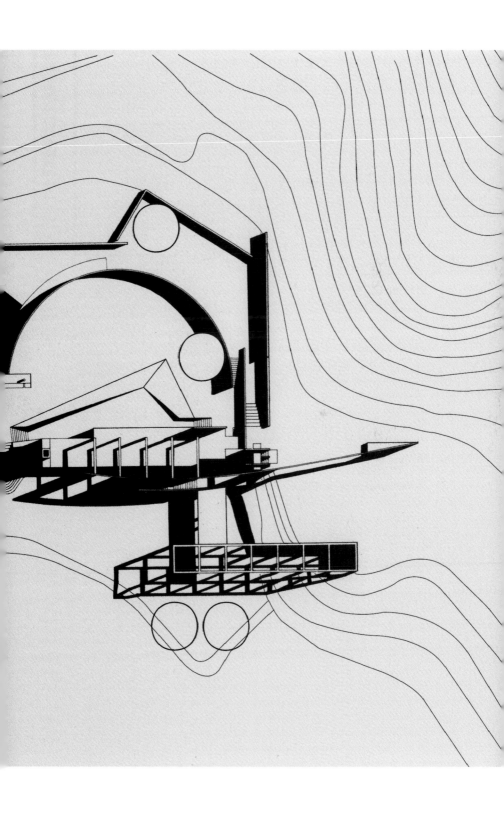

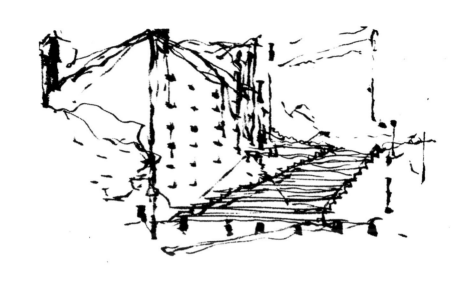

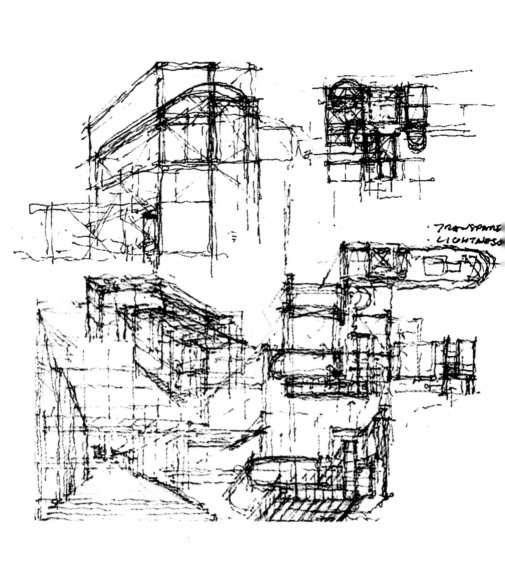

·TRANSPAR[
·LICHTNESO

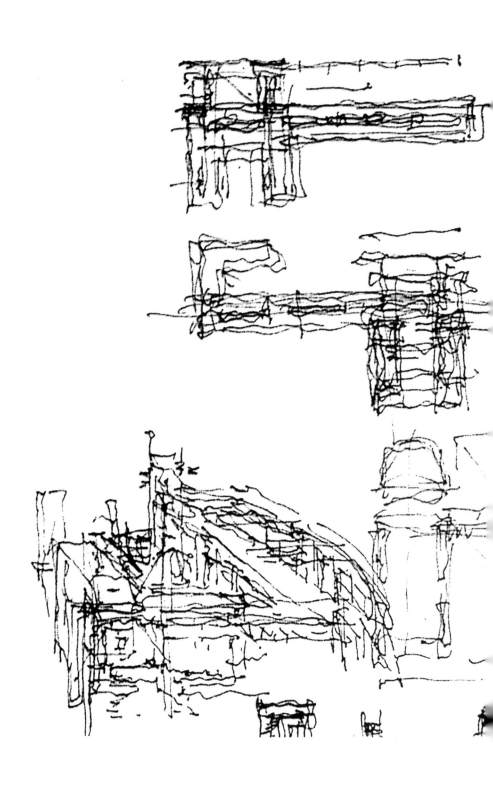

GALLERY ANA

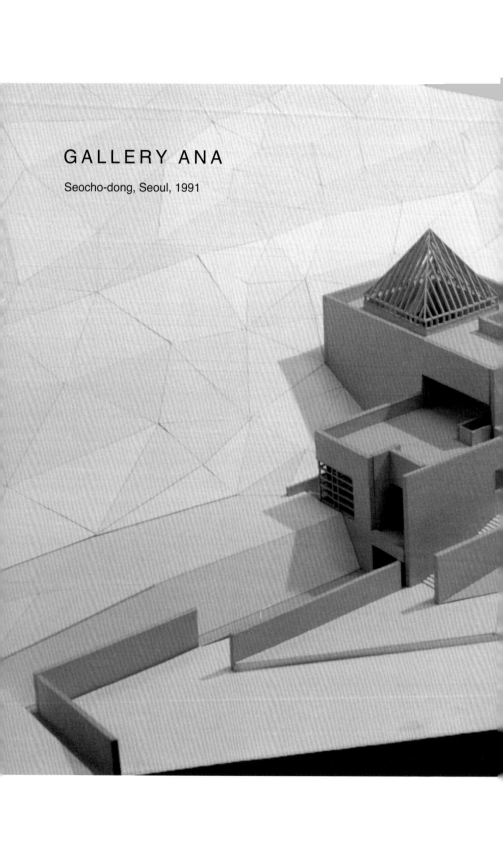

GALLERY ANA

Seocho-dong, Seoul, 1991

The site is close to a major metropolis area, yet it combines the elements of urban and rural characteristics. In the rear of this mountainous site exists a fairly dense forest that seems to absorb the energy emanating from the city. The key to the design solution was to anchor the city's vitality in the rusticity of the site and in the process allow the building's own dynamism to filter and transform this energy into something more refined. Hierarchical composition of building volume leads easily to an entry sequence that continues through the exhibition

space out to the outdoor sunken court. The other nearby support facilities, including a cafe, a design shop and a restaurant, fall effortlessly along this sequence that is reinforced by the linear composition along the geographical formation. Juxtaposition and contrast between the built structure and the nature provide the building with a sense of place lacking in this urban oasis.

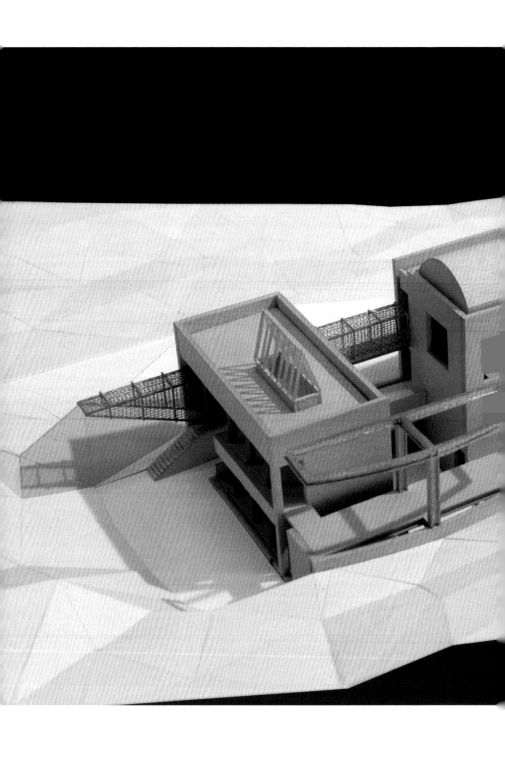

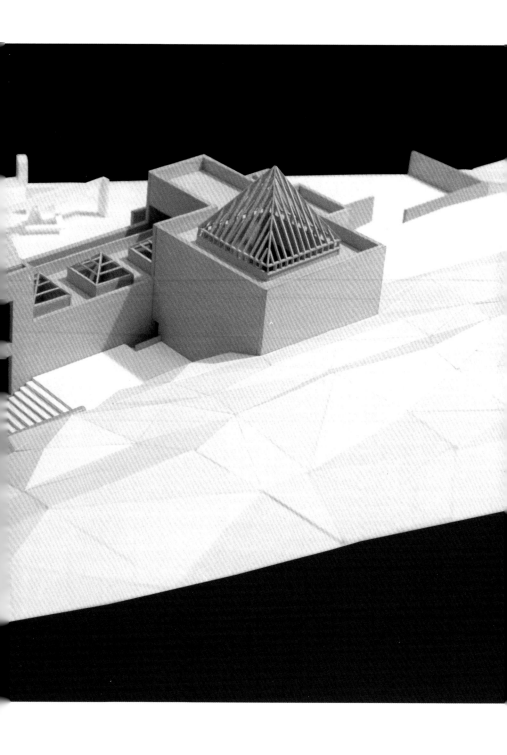

GALLERY GWANGJU

GALLERY GWANGJU

Gwangju-si, Gyeonggi-do, 2001

The site commands a picturesque view with an access road on its vicinity and a stream across the valley. As part of the master plan for an outdoor sculpture park, the project called for the design of an art museum. The outdoor bridges and terraces were introduced not only as a means to connect the two buildings but also to harmonize the relationship between the buildings and the site.

JEJU MUSEUM

JEJU MUSEUM

Jeju-do, 2013

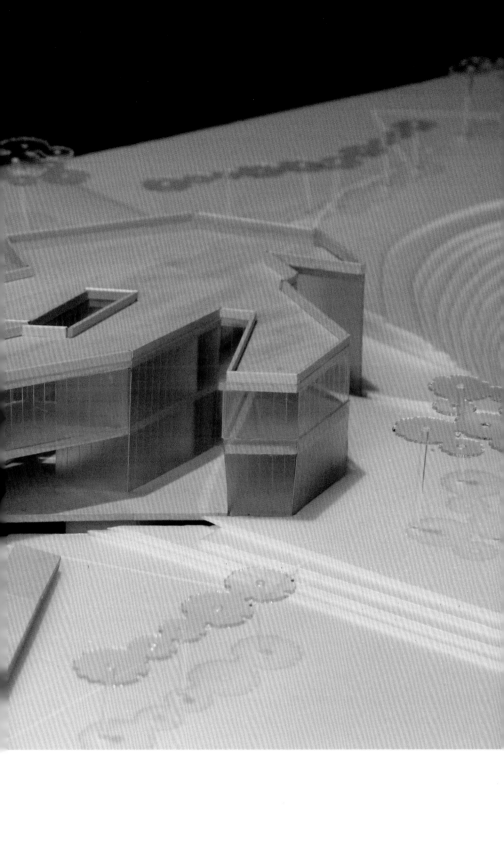

The setting for this museum is an island located in the southern part of the Korean peninsula. The free-formed mass whose plan induces an uninterrupted, continuous traffic flow inside the museum, takes a form after a local phenomenon with a core in the center which turns out to be one of the most effective exhibition space layout plans. Its dynamic form is based on the frequented image of clouds hung on top of the volcanic mountain Halla in the island.

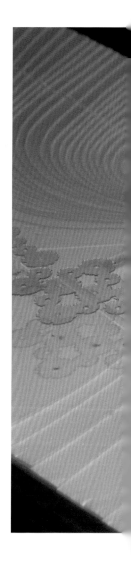

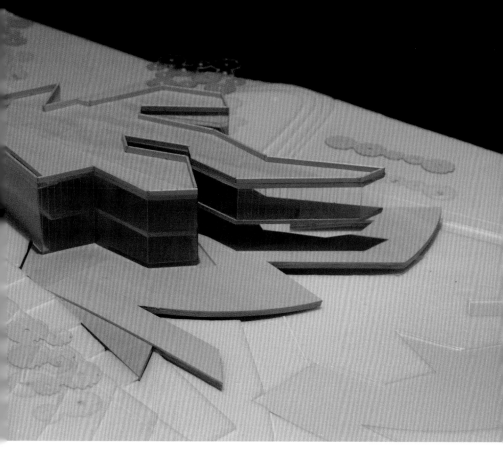

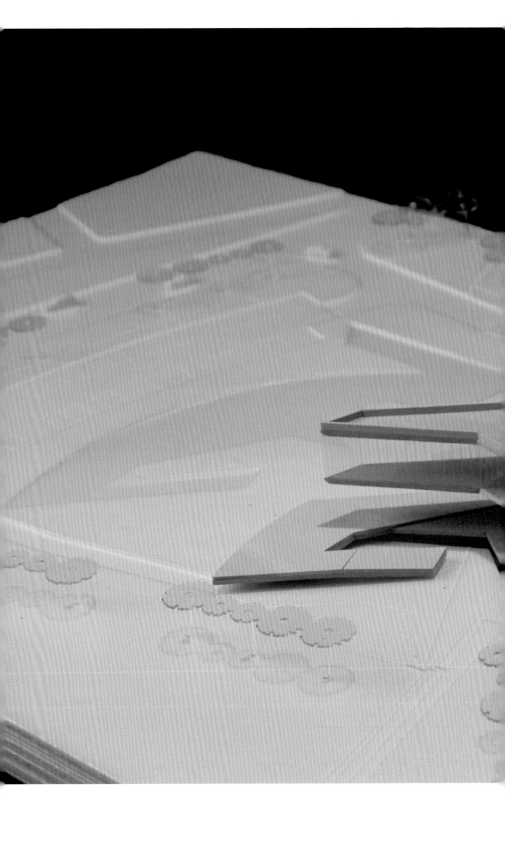

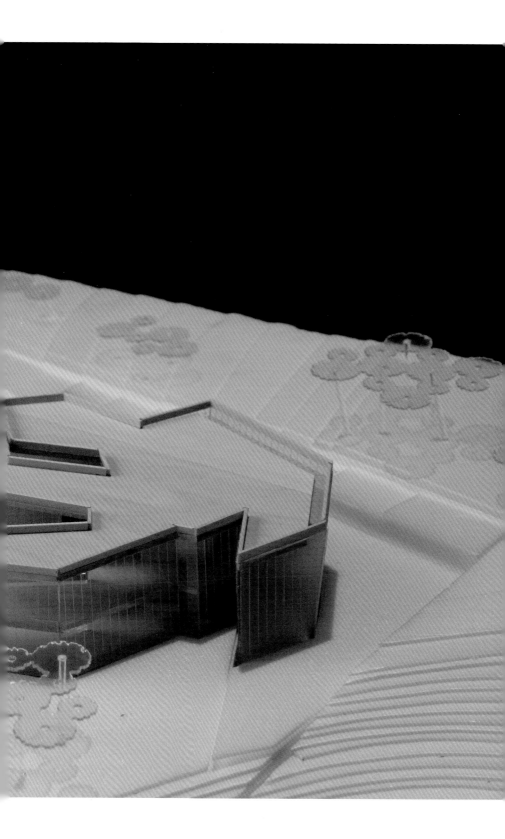

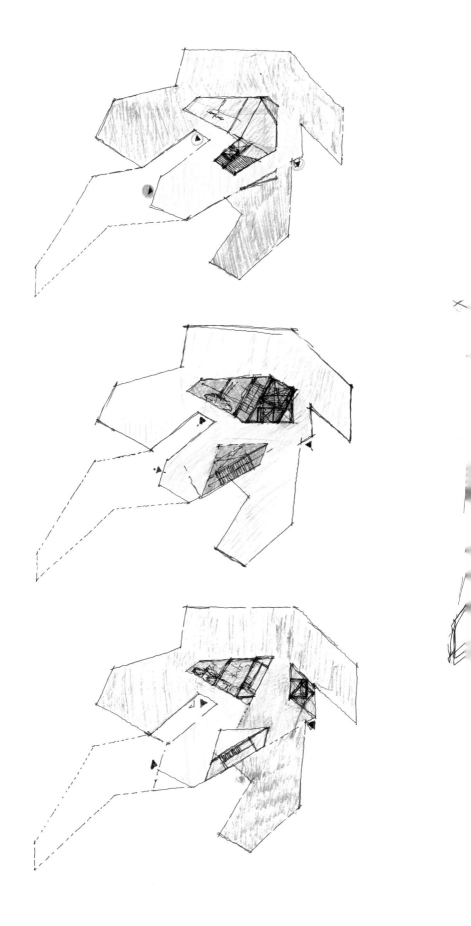

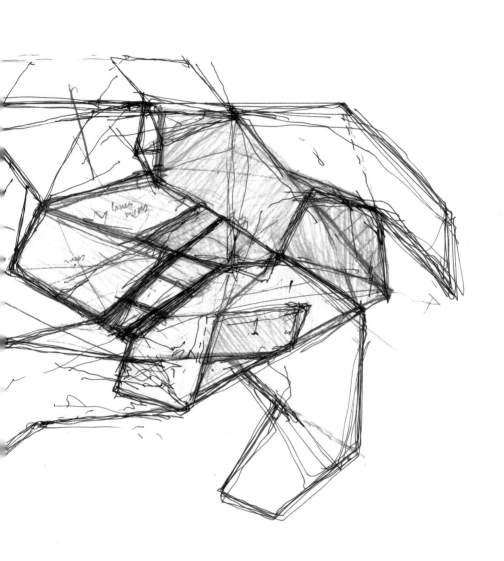

GRAND EGYPTIAN MUSEUM

GRAND EGYPTIAN MUSEUM

Giza, Egypt, 2002

Throughout the history of mankind, countless civilizations have risen and fallen in many parts of the world. Among those who strove to achieve even higher realms of cultural, physical and spiritual enlightenment, no other civilization can claim to have matched or exceeded Egypt in its scale, diversity, sophistication and grandeur. Hence, the International Competition for the Grand Egyptian Museum (GEM) provides a rare and exciting opportunity to design a place that will house artifacts representing not only the great achievements of Egypt but also the human spirit itself for generations to come. GEM is to be a gift from the people of Egypt to the people around the globe to share, to appreciate and to inspire all that is noble and enduring in people no matter what its color or creed.

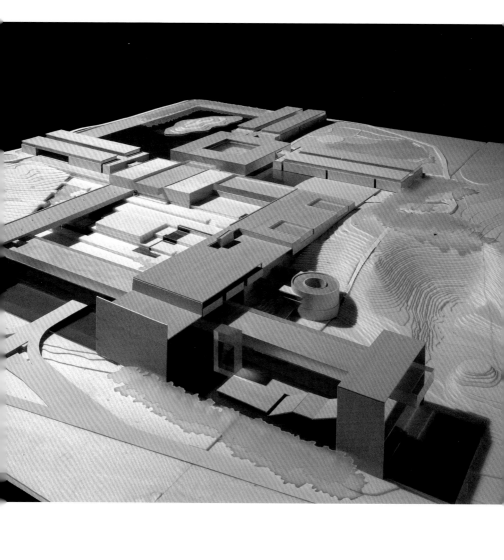

In designing the GEM, care was taken not to compete with the strong image of the nearby pyramids. Instead, GEM was conceived to achieve its own architectural stature that complements the pyramids. If pyramids are a concentration of power expressed as singular objects, GEM is designed so the visitors and users can feel

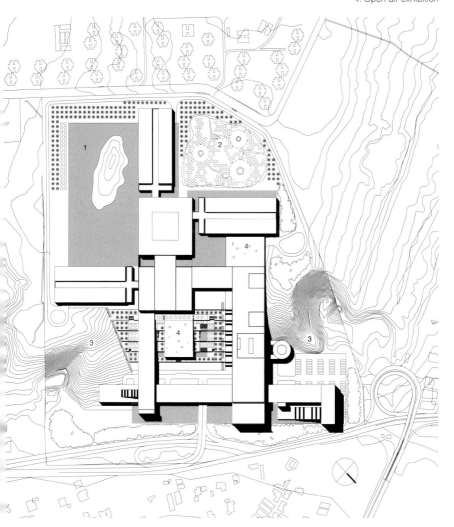

1. Nile park
2. Theme park
3. Dunal park
4. Open-air exhibition

the gentle emanation of energy that springs from it and spreads through the architectural spaces onto the land that surrounds them. Put another way, pyramids may be said
to emphasize the vertical and static energy. In contrast, GEM can be understood as a
horizontal movement of energy.

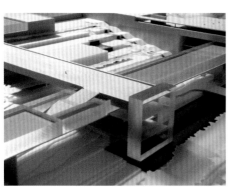

 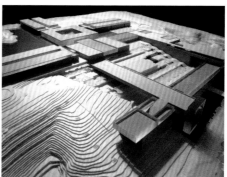

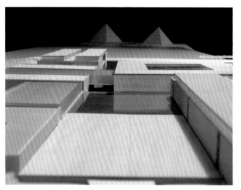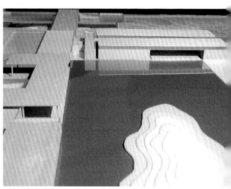

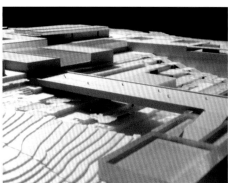

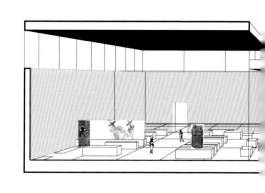

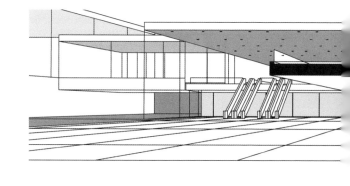

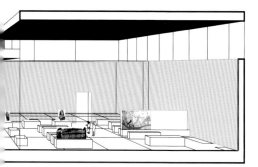

Permanent exhibition

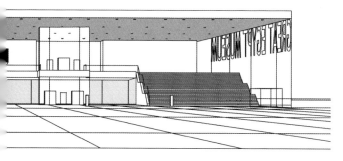

Main entrance hall

NATIONAL MUSEUM OF
MODERN & CONTEMPORARY ART

NATIONAL MUSEUM OF
MODERN & CONTEMPORARY ART

Sogyeok-dong, Seoul, 2010

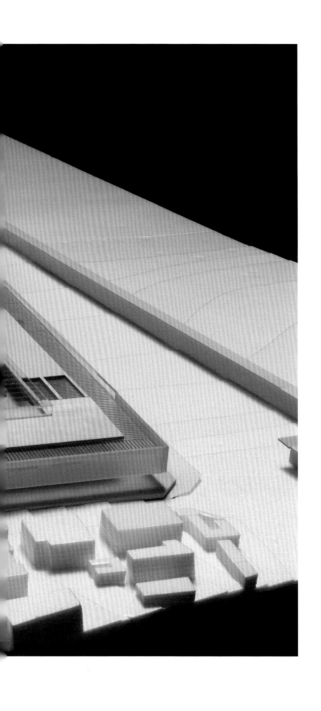

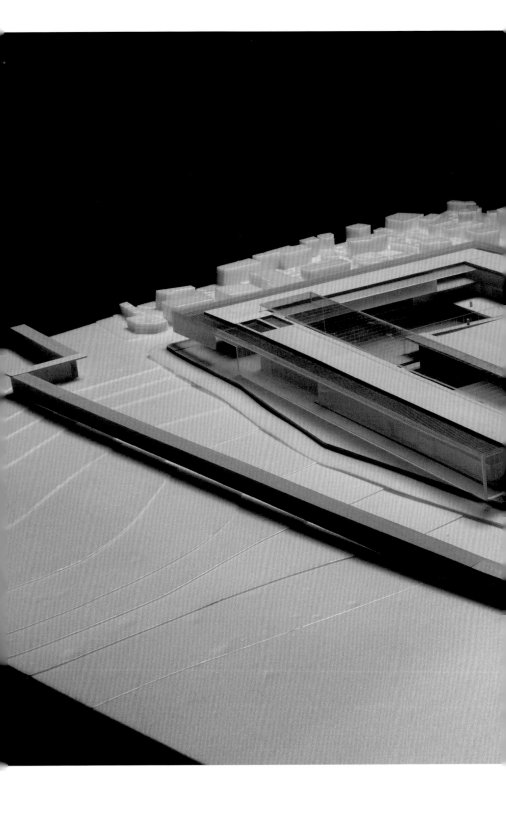

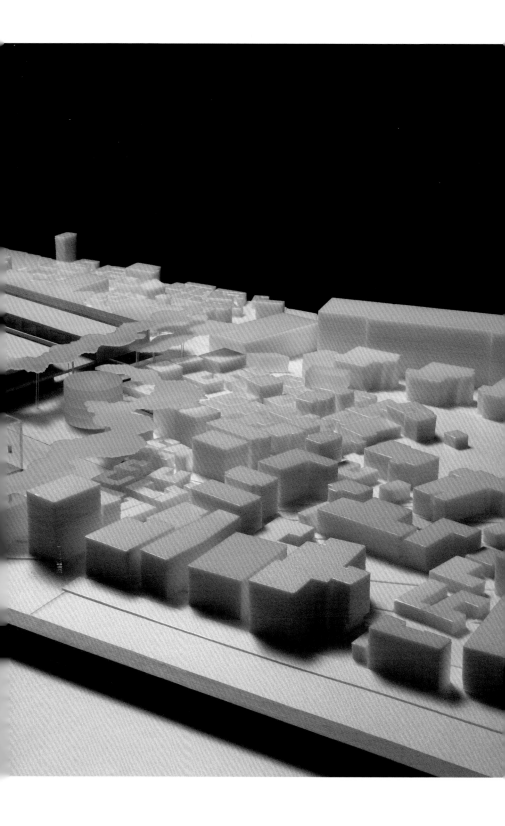

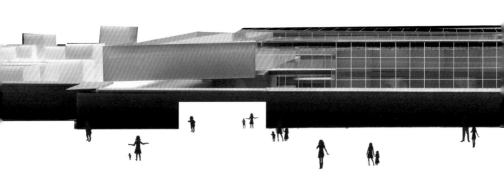

Classic Korean palace architecture is organized around a series of strict geometric principles that find their roots in Chinese city planning of 2000 years ago; these are embedded in the design of Gyeongbok-gung Palace. The concept of walled enclosures, courtyards and the replication of rectilinear forms that signal hierarchy and privacy and the specific North/South orientation of the palace are all present. Now a public museum, the design of the palace complex still resonates with its visitors.

The design approach to the National Museum of Modern & Contemporary Art (MMCA) complex takes its cues from these historic planning principles in order to create a dialogue between the two complexes. In scale and orientation, the new MMCA building echoes the Geungjeongjeon Hall of Gyeongbok-gung Palace and courtyard within the palace.

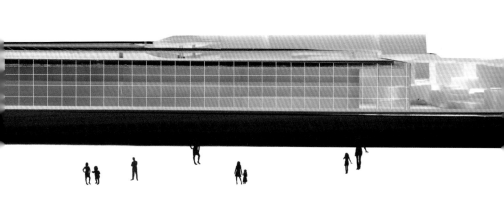

The walled enclosure remains an organizing idea for the new complex. The wall which makes up the three sides of the MMCA complex, however, is no longer a barrier; the wall becomes a spatial anchor that links the complex to the street and to the palace. Much of the first floor is permeable to public inner courtyard and the rooftop sculpture garden and this flow connects with the outlying pattern of streets and alleyways. The spatial blocks define the media center, the administrative offices and the existing landmark building.

One of the major challenges of the site is this existing landmark building. While historically significant, the building does not relate to its surroundings and is not a particularly useful structure within the museum complex as it stands. By enclosing the building in glass and incorporating it as a piece of the "wall," the building takes on a dual function: one of design and one of history.

- Weight, Depth, Volume 중세, 톤, 부피감
  노개 재호 강조
- 공료양 측면에서의 강조

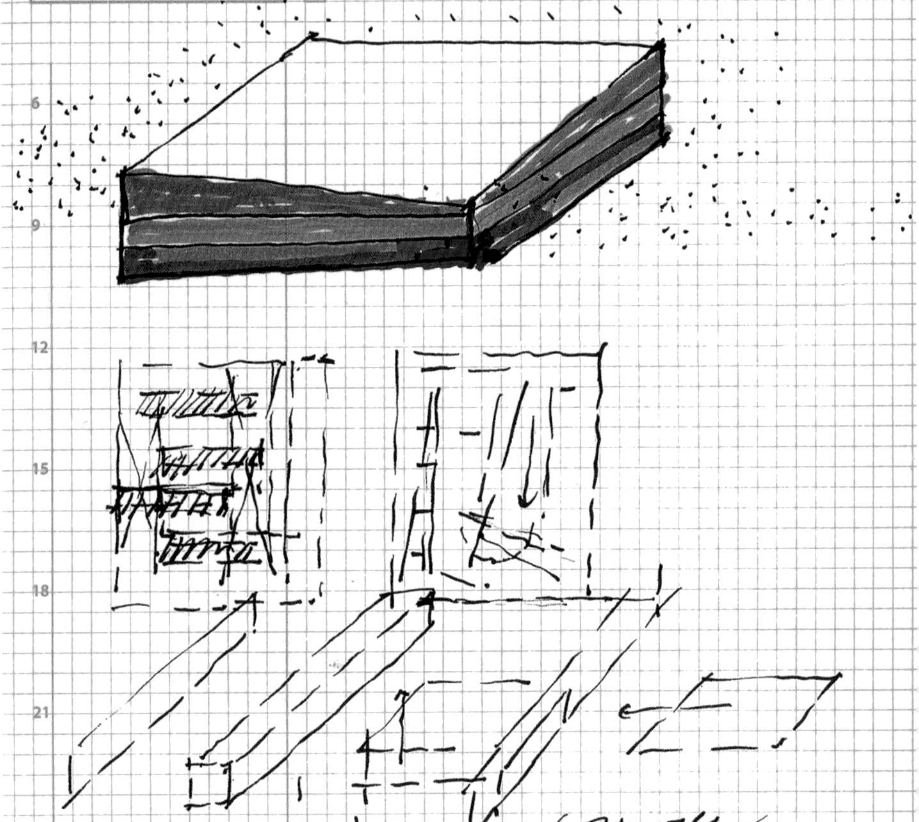

SOLID / VOID
opaque / transparency
spaced / movement
LIGHT

Serenity
無 (Silence 空
Clarity / Order
convivity
DENSITY

DYNAMIC
LIGHT / AIRY
Sharp / Pnesthie
mobile / multi-
Directional

BAEKSUN SAINT PAUL'S HOUSE

BAEKSUN
SAINT PAUL'S HOUSE

Samgeo-dong, Gwangju-si, 2000

This project was an addition to the original building that was located in the foothills of a mountain.
The program called for living facilities for mentally
disabled children and offices for administrative
staff. The second floor of the building consisted
of apartment units that were to be used as a train-
ing center for the students in preparation for an
independent life as adults.

Because the main users are disabled individuals,
a clear line of circulation, sufficient natural light,
and a comfortable atmosphere were the priorities
reflected in the building design.

CHEONJUNGSA CULTURAL INSTITUTE

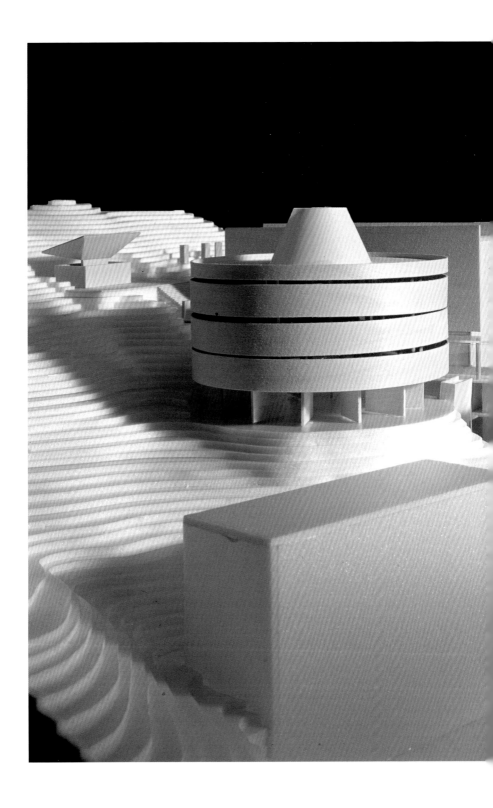

CHEONJUNGSA CULTURAL INSTITUTE

Jeongneung-dong, Seoul, 1999

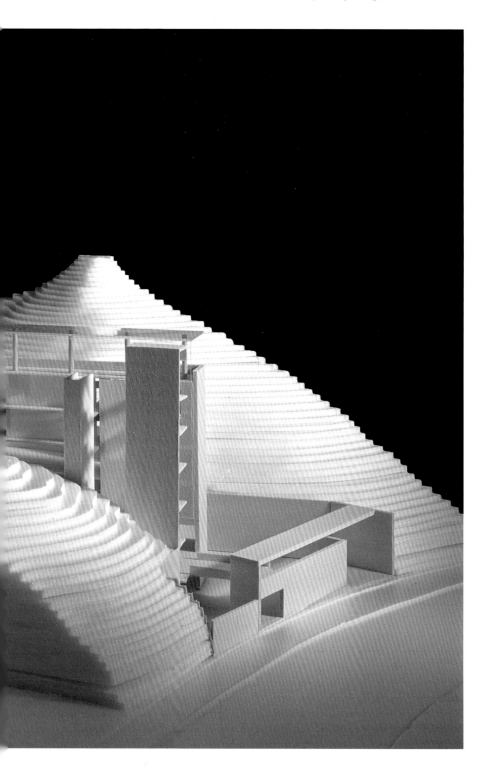

The competition called for a modern reinterpretation of a temple and a charnel house. In order to adapt to the steepness of the existing topography while minimizing further destruction of the hill, the recti-linear volume and the cylindrical tower were placed between two valleys and on the upper part of the gentle hill in the site, respectively.

As for the circulation, a set of vertical stair towers were proposed alongside the rectilinear building, not only for functional reasons but also as symbolic objects that would signify the connection between the departed and the living.

Another set of continuous stairs on the ground level, extending from the entrance court all the way to the new temple on top of a hill at the back of the site, was included to express the seemingly eternal distance between heaven and earth. As far as the connections are concerned, a set of bridges were proposed as primary mode of con-nection between buildings.

HAEIN BUDDHIST CULTURAL CENTER

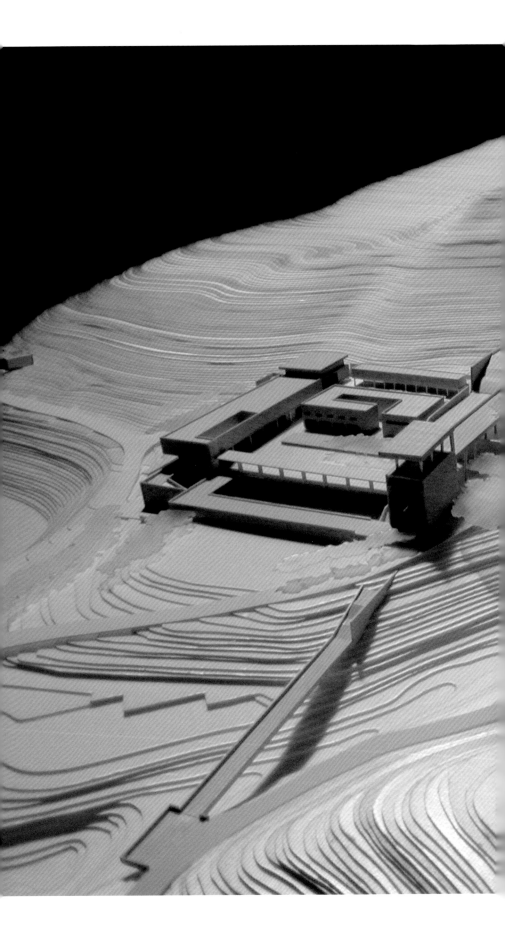

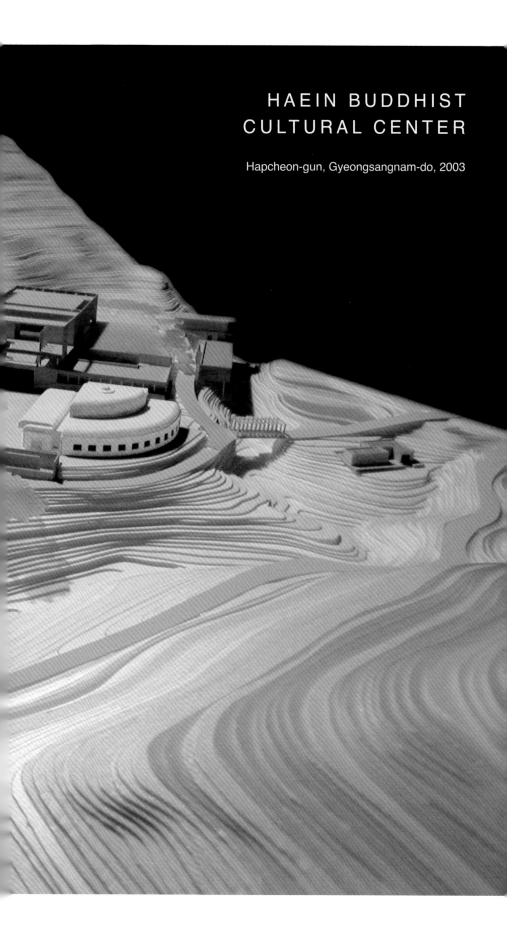

HAEIN BUDDHIST CULTURAL CENTER

Hapcheon-gun, Gyeongsangnam-do, 2003

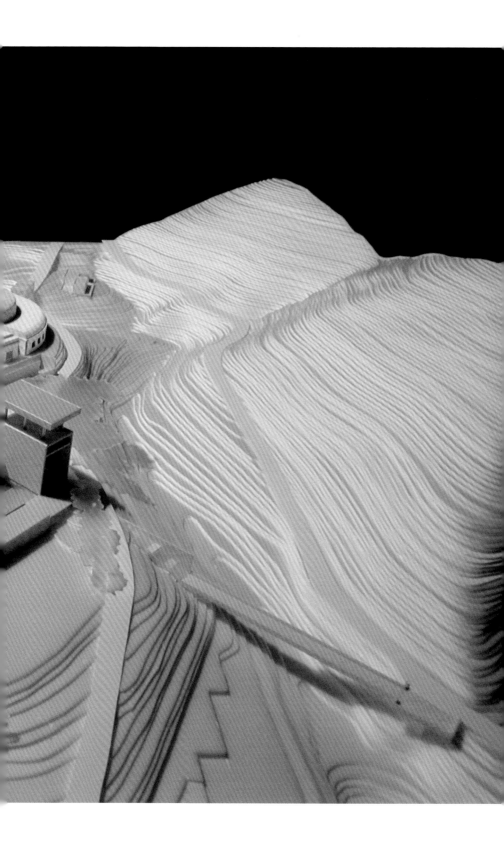

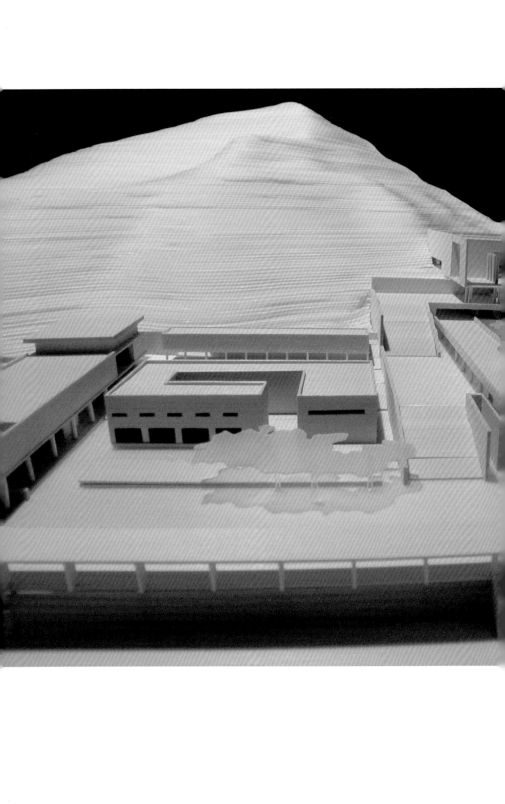

In designing the ceremonial and cultural seminary spaces for Haeinsa which is located in the mountain Gaya, the natural topography was to be respected as much as possible without impairing the site's existing geography. From this point of view, the direction of the design was to revive the surrounding nature by creating a reciprocated relationship between man and nature.

Specifically, the design intention was to create an elegant and delicate religious space that harmonizes the various elements of Korean traditional temple design. The overall space distribution follows the natural topography of the lower and higher part of the site in the architectural scheme where an entry plaza, a ceremonial hall, and worship area have their respective place in architectural sequence.

GWANGYANG COMMUNITY CENTER

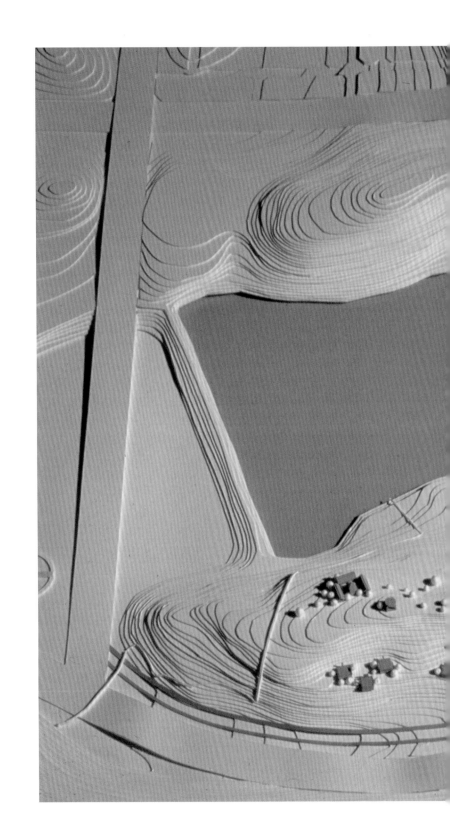

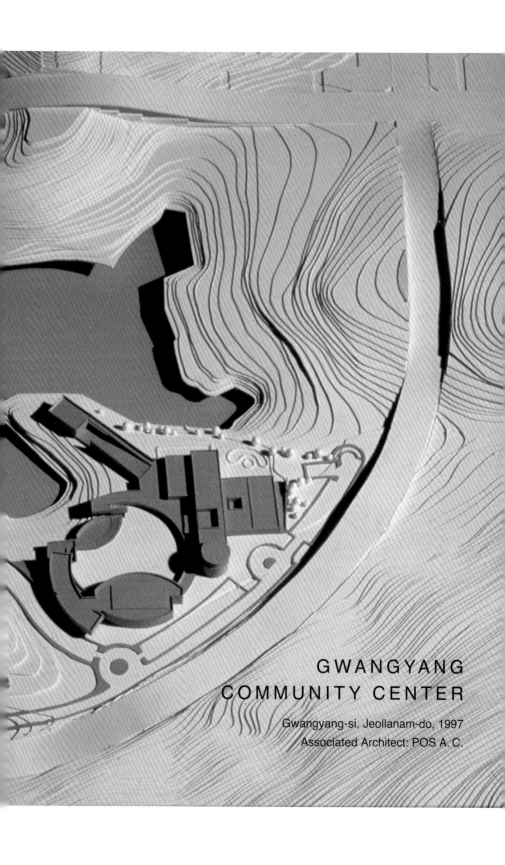

GWANGYANG
COMMUNITY CENTER

Gwangyang-si, Jeollanam-do, 1997
Associated Architect: POS A. C.

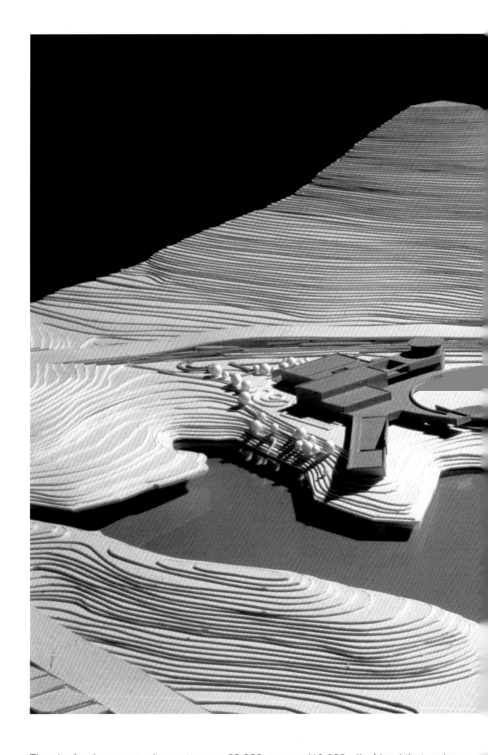

The site for the community center was 30,000 *pyeong* (10,000m²) of land that embraced the mountain, water and spectacular views. The intended programs for the center were cultural and sports facilities. The main concept was to create a central courtyard space to bring the natural flow of the mountains and the water into the site. Inside the courtyard

space, a large grass field was planned to provide a public plaza that would unify buildings of different scales and functions. Sports facilities and a gallery were to share an open space in between. The design intention was to connect each facility for the sake of convenience while maintaining independent flow of movement.

MAIN LIBRARY ARCADE, SNU

MAIN LIBRARY ARCADE, SEOUL NATIONAL UNIVERSITY
RENOVATION

Daehak-dong, Seoul, 2006

Ample lighting, bold floor patterns, as well as a floating cafe and set of billboards hung from the ceiling are some of the main elements implemented to give a new life to what used to be a dark and old arcaded outdoor corridor under the main library of Seoul National University. The use of painted glass walls and a series of vertical lights housed in the etched glass covers, helps to create an environment full of light and energy. Modulation between horizontal and vertical elements as well as the texture of building materials was carefully orchestrated to create a sense of rhythm that accentuates a dynamic flow in the arcaded corridor.

GWANAK SQUARE, SNU

GWANAK SQUARE, SEOUL NATIONAL UNIVERSITY

Daehak-dong, Seoul, 2012

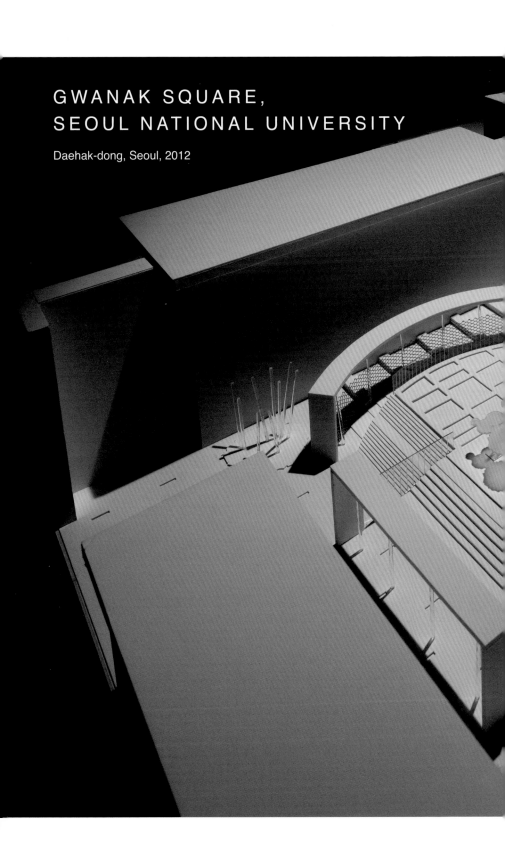

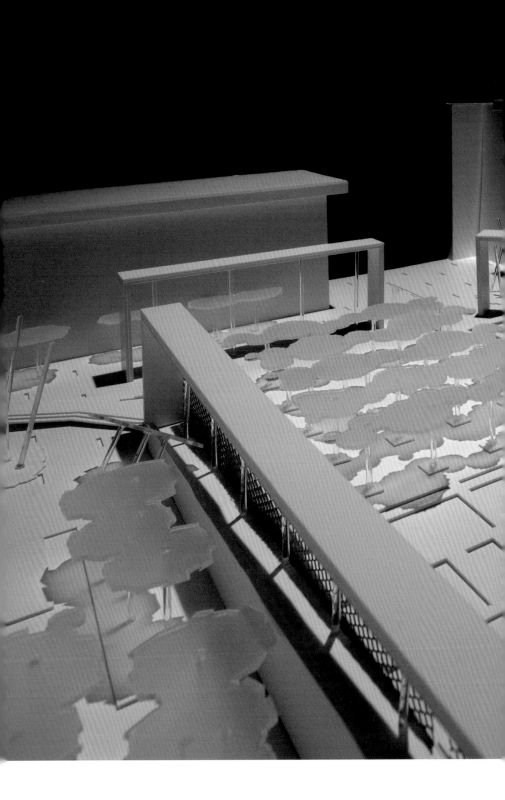

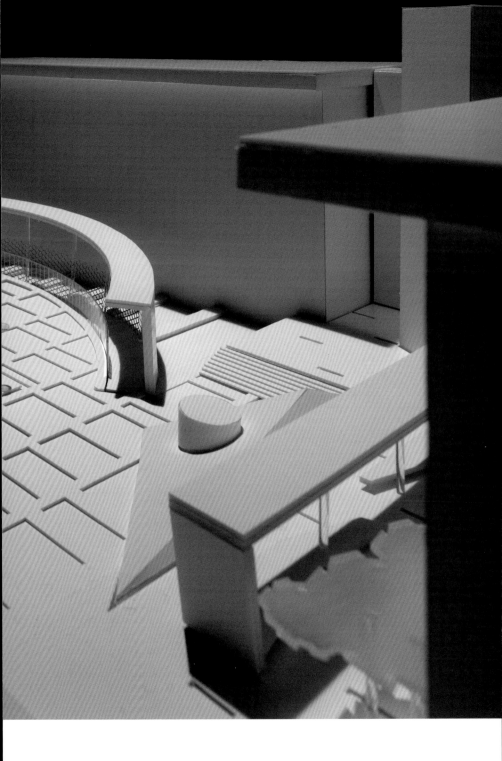

The design intention for Gwanak Square stems from the desire to replace the old square with a new one that would provide a wide, open outdoor space with plenty of green land-scape to facilitate foot traffic in all directions and serve as an outdoor forum for students. The new square not only plays the role of a landmark within the engineering campus by es-

tablishing itself as an outdoor connector between the main library and the college of engineering, but also provides a generous setting for a meeting and resting place for students. With the diverse choice of circulation paths open to all directions, it can be a place of rest and meditation at the same time.

DESIGN

Wire Mesh Table, 2006

Wire Mesh Shelving, 2006

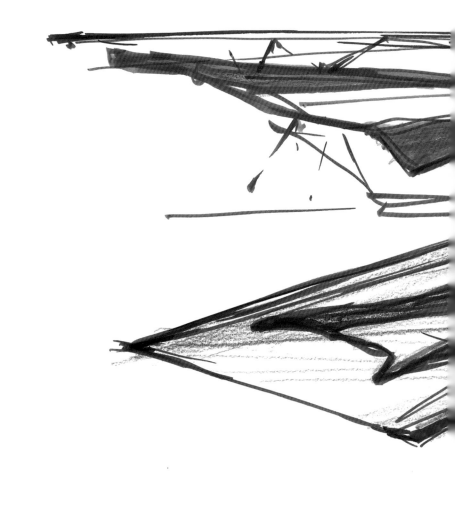

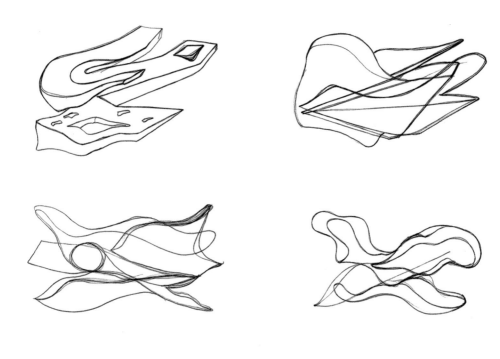

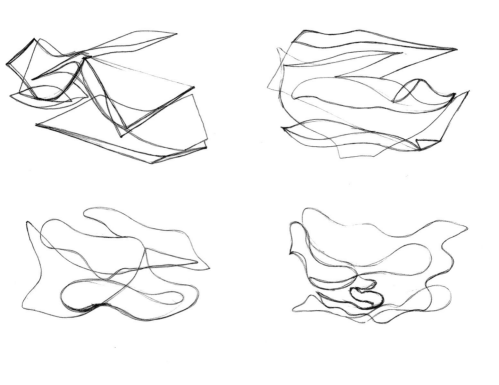

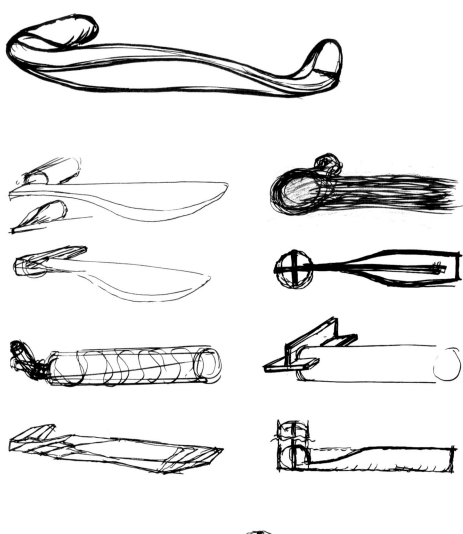

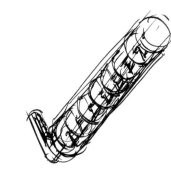

Door Handle, 2008

Exhibition Booth, 2009

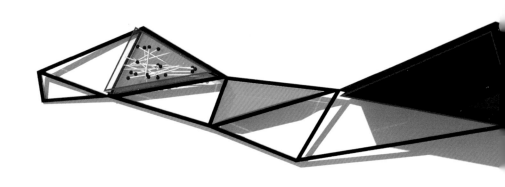

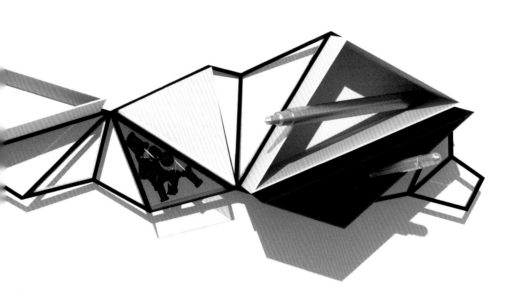

Space Organizer, 2008

DUNAM CHOI

Born in Korea in 1953, DuNam Choi is an architect, painter and professor at Seoul National University in Seoul, Korea. He received his Bachelor of Fine Art at University of California, Berkeley and Master of Architecture at GSD, Harvard University.

As an educator and architect, Choi has been involved with academia and architectural practice for over twenty five years in Korea and the U.S. Currently teaching at the Department of Architecture in Seoul National University, he has exhibited and lectured extensively, including an exhibition at GSD and a lecture on New Design in Seoul at a public forum of AIA New York Chapter.

Choi began his career in the United States, working at KPF and Woo and Williams from 1984 to 1988 and then directing an architectural design office of his own named DuNam Choi Associates from 1988 to 1996 in California. His work has been honorably recognized and awarded by Progressive Architecture, and the Architectural Foundation of San Francisco in the U.S. He has also won Korea Institute of Architecture Award for his design of Gallery Samtuh in 1998. His public posts includes membership in the presidential commission on architectural policy in Korea. As a member of American Institute of Architects, he has completed many architectural projects that range from residential to commercial and cultural such as the Hannam-dong House, the Buam-dong House, Joil Building and Gallery Samtuh. His work has been published a number of times in architectural magazines and publications including *Award Winning Architecture* by Prestel.

www.dca-snu.co.kr / duchoi5301@gmail.com

CREDITS

EDITORIAL STAFF

YOULHWADANG: Soojung Yi, Mi Kyung Kong
TAW : Wonhee Lee, Bora Lee, Sahar H. Motlagh, Jiyoung Kim

PHOTO

PAINTING, 2013
Andy H. Jung

BUAM-DONG HOUSE
Kim Jongoh + Lee Jonggeun

HANNAM-DONG HOUSE
Kim Jongoh

PYEONGCHANG-DONG HOUSE
Kim Jae Kyeong

P-PROJECT
DuNam Choi

RFB HOUSE
Kim Jae Kyeong

YANGPYEONG HOUSE
Kim Jae Kyeong

YONGIN HOUSE
Park Wan Soon

JOAN-RI HOUSE
Kim Jae Kyeong

GLASS HOUSE
Kim Jongoh

YEONHEE-DONG HOUSE
Kim Jongoh

ITAEWON HOUSE
Namgung Seon

LEE HOUSE
Kim Jae Kyeong

SEOCHO-DONG HOUSE
Lim Chung Eui

JEJU-DO HOUSE
Lim Chung Eui

JOIL BUILDING
Kim Yong Kwan

MAYA BUILDING
Kim Jongoh

YOUNGCHANG PRINTING
Kim Jongoh

SAMPYO BUILDING
Kim Jae Kyeong

NEW KOREA COUNTRY CLUB
Kim Jongoh

NAMSAN BUILDING
Kim Jongoh

WEDGE
Kim Jongoh

YOUNG PROJECT
Kim Dohyeong

CHOI'S HARDWARE COMPANY
Kim Jae Kyeong

SHANGHAI INTERNATIONAL CENTER
Samwoo Architects

SAEGANG BUILDING
Lim Chung Eui

GALLERY SAMTUH
Lim Chung Eui + Kim Yong Kwan

HANGIL ART SPACE 3
Kim Jongoh

GALLERY SEOJONG
Kim Yong Kwan

ART CENTER
Lim Chung Eui

OPEN AIR MUSEUM
Lim Chung Eui, Gerald Ratto, Henrik Kam

GALLERY ANA
Lim Chung Eui

GALLERY GWANGJU
Namgung Seon

JEJU MUSEUM
TAW

GRAND EGYPTIAN MUSEUM
Kim Jae Kyeong

NATIONAL MUSEUM OF MODERN &
CONTEMPORARY ART
Kim Jae Kyeong

BAEKSUN SAINT PAUL'S HOUSE
Kim Jongoh

CHEONJUNGSA CULTURAL INSTITUTE
Kim Jongoh

HAEIN BUDDHIST CULTURAL CENTER
Kim Dohyeong

GWANGYANG COMMUNITY CENTER
Kim Jae Kyeong

MAIN LIBRARY ARCADE,
SEOUL NATIONAL UNIVERSITY
Kim Jae Kyeong

GWANAK SQUARE,
SEOUL NATIONAL UNIVERSITY
Kim Jae Kyeong

DUNAM CHOI, LYON, 2009.
Daesung Kim

TEXT

Jong Soung Kimm, "Foreword," 2013.
Yi Euisung, "Dunam Choi's Houses": From *Space Magazine*, November 2012.
Peter Choi, "Total Design": From *Space Magazine*, November 2012.
DuNam Choi, "Toward an Architecture of Substance and Gravity": From *Korean Architects*, October 1993.

DUNAM CHOI ARCHITECT
1987-2013

초판1쇄발행 2014년 1월 6일
발행인 李起雄
발행처 悅話堂
경기도 파주시 광인사길 25 (문발동 520-10) 파주출판도시
TEL 031-955-7000, **FAX** 031-955-7010
www.youlhwadang.co.kr yhdp@youlhwadang.co.kr
등록번호 제 10-74호
등록일자 1971년 7월 2일

인쇄 제책 (주)상지사피앤비

DUNAM CHOI ARCHITECT © 2014 by DuNam Choi
Published by Youlhwadang Publishers.
Paju Bookcity, Gwanginsa-gil 25 (520-10 Munbal-dong),
Paju-si, Gyeonggi-do, Korea
Printed in Korea.

ISBN 978-89-301-0458-6 93610

120,000 KRW

이 도서의 국립중앙도서관 출판시도서목록(CIP)은
서지정보유통지원시스템 홈페이지(http://seoji.nl.go.kr)와
국가자료공동목록시스템(http://www.nl.go.kr/kolisnet)에서
이용하실 수 있습니다.(CIP제어번호 : CIP2014000580)